Bicycles, Donkeys, Deserts and Fish

The Memoirs and Memories of John M Macleod, Balallan

Introduction

In 1984 when I retired from teaching my thoughts were centred on enjoying the rest of my life on my favourite hobby of angling – both fresh water and sea angling.

There is no dearth of angling opportunities in Lewis and sometimes I set off very early in the mornings but this did not prevent my wife Margaret from preparing my breakfast and sending me off with a good luck kiss which invariably worked!

In preparing this book I got help and invaluable advice from Margaret and from our three daughters Annabel, Helen and Patricia, all of whom are pictured above. Helen, residing in Laxay and thus within easy reach, bore the brunt of the work involved!

I am most grateful to them all.

John M Macleod

First published in Great Britain in 2009 by John M Macleod
ISBN 978-0-9561934-0-7
Copyright John M. Macleod 2009
Thug Comhairle nan Leabhraichean tabhartas barantais dhan fhoillsichear airson nan cuibhreannan Gàidhlig san leabhar seo.
Edited and prepared for publication by Intermedia Services, Stornoway
Printed and bound by Gomer Press Ltd, Llandysul, Ceredigion

Contents

Preface

Sometimes it pays to play by the rules, sometimes it is better to defy your rulers! Two episodes from my memories will show you what I mean.

In 1946 I was still with the RAF in East Africa and I was due to accompany an RAF cricket tour in the plane I was maintaining. Cricket games were played at Aden in Southern Arabia and then we flew on to Mogadishu in what is now Somalia for refuelling en route to Kenya for more games. When a petrol bowser had finished the refuelling, I opened the four draining cocks underneath the tanks to drain away any water which had condensed there since the previous refuelling. Many mechanics overlooked this instruction as usually the amount of water forming in the tanks was negligible, but fortunately I did not.

The fuel cocks were locked with copper wire which had to be cut starting at No.1 and the tap opened. This procedure was followed with the other three drain-cocks. The way to differentiate water from petrol was to let what emerged from the tap flow into the palm of your hand and if it was water it would bubble and if it was petrol it would not.

After the refuelling bowser had topped up the four tanks which could hold 802 gallons all told, I started the checking procedure and found to my alarm that it was water – in considerable quantity – that was flowing from the tanks.

I turned all the taps off and went to find the Station Engineering Officer. When he came along and saw the amount of liquid on the concrete hard-standing he told me to turn on the taps again. He tested each tank and immediately agreed that it was water and not petrol that was emerging. He told me to close all the taps and soon an empty bowser came and sucked the tanks dry.

Another fuel bowser was standing by and filled the tanks up again. Before take-off I asked the Engineering Officer to confirm that all we had in our tanks was petrol. When we did check we found that it was petrol that emerged from the tanks. As petrol is lighter than water it rises to the top and so if we had taken off without the check being done, we would probably have flown for some time but not for the three and three quarter hours it took us to reach Eastleigh near Nairobi – there would have been another mystery air-crash in the jungles of Africa. The message from this is: "Always go by the book!"

It turned out that the fuel was transported to Mogadishu in 50 gallon drums in trucks driven by Italian POWs – some of the drivers used to sell some of it on the way north and top up the drums with water!

Balallan in the old days, looking east

However, there are times when it is better to play the game differently.

On the troopship out to Egypt during the war, our dining room was organised in this way. We sat at benches, ten on each side and an NCO at the top dispensed the meals on plates which were passed down to the unfortunates who sat at the far end of the benches, of which I was one. By giving smaller portions to us he was sure there would be more than ample left in the urn to provide a good meal for himself and his cronies beside him. One day I got annoyed at the meagre portions we at the lower end of the table received and I told my mates not to touch theirs as I was going to protest once everyone was served.

I took my plate hidden behind my back and walked up to the top of the table. "Corporal," I said "Are you not supposed to serve the food in equal portions?"

"Of course and that's what I'm doing," he barked.

"OK, Corporal, will you then exchange your plate with mine?" I said as I produced it from behind my back.

He flew into a rage but then the Orderly Officer fortuitously appeared and asked what the trouble was. I explained to him and when he saw the difference in the contents of the two plates he said: "Corporal, exchange your plate with the airman's." As I arrived at the bottom of the table there were cheers from my neighbours. Next day there was a different NCO serving the food!

From Shakespeare's
As You Like It
(Act II Scene VII)

JAQUES

All the world's a stage

And all the men and women merely players;

And one man in his time plays many parts

His acts being seven ages.

At first the infant mewling and puking in the nurse's arms.

And then the whining schoolboy, with his satchel and shining morning face, creeping like snail unwillingly to school.

And then the lover sighing like furnace, with a woeful ballad made to his mistress' eyebrows.

Then a soldier full of strange oaths and bearded like the pard, jealous in honour, sudden and quick to quarrel.

Then the Justice in fair round belly with eyes severe full of wise saws and modern instances.

The sixth age shifts into the slippered pantaloon with spectacles on nose; his youthful hose a world too wide for his shrunk shank.

Last scene of all that ends this strange eventful history is second childishness and mere oblivion – sans teeth, sans eyes, sans taste, sans everything.

Chapter 1

Circumstantial Evidence and the Repeal of Sammy's Law

On 7th February 1924, I was born at 1 Clunepark Street, Port Glasgow but as far as I know there was no civic reception to mark the occasion! When I was three months old I decided to go to Lewis as I was not enamoured with life in the Lowlands. Fortunately, my parents concurred with my wishes and we set off overland by train and overseas by the 'Sheila' to our new home at 50 Balallan. Apparently it was a very stormy night when we crossed the Minch, but despite the heavy seas I was not seasick – or so they told me – nor did I ever suffer from 'mal de mer' or 'cur na mara' as it is called in Celtic circles – perhaps the reason being my early initiation to the Cuan Sgìth – the Minch.

The Sheila lying at the pier in Kyleakin

Incidentally on the night the 'Iolaire' was lost, January 1, 1919, the 'Sheila' – pictured above – sailed safely from Kyle of Lochalsh to Stornoway having been overtaken by the 'Iolaire' which ended up on the Beasts of Holm with such heavy loss of life. It is tragic that she didn't follow the course of the 'Sheila'.

After settling in Lewis the first thing I remember was my maternal grandfather, Iain an Tàilleir, Airidhbhruaich, presenting me in 1926 with a beautiful Highland calf, which I cherished until it sprouted the most hideous pair of horns one could imagine! In fact, one of those fearsome horns nearly gouged out one of my father's eyes when he was tethering it in the byre, but in due course the family were able to enjoy many a creamy bowl of milk from that horny, shaggy beast!

When I was about three years old an aunt and uncle home on holiday from Glasgow presented me with a rubber ball, smaller than a football but larger than any ball I had ever seen. During the summer I used to play with it in the field beside our house. On one occasion my father and my uncle Murdo who later became a Church of Scotland Minister, were installing a wooden gate at the road side of the field. My mother came to call us all to lunch and typically I required a second call before I complied. After lunch my father and my uncle went back to their gate-installing and I went back to my footballing. In a short while my father came to ask me what I had done with the screw-nails they had left where they had been working on the gate. I truthfully pleaded innocence but the case against me was strong – viz: when my father and uncle went in for lunch there were screw-nails beside the gate; I went in for lunch later than they did and when we all came out together there were no screw-nails beside the gate; ergo as there were no other human beings around, I was found guilty and punishment was summarily administered; my father put me across his knee and smacked my bare bottom. Again I was asked what I had done with the screw-nails and again I denied knowledge of their existence. I can now understand the frustration caused by their disappearance as this entailed a trip to Stornoway to replace them – there was no ironmonger in Balallan.

Earlier in the Spring, my father had been on the moor gathering sheep for lambing and he found the nest of a goose in which there were four eggs. He took them home in his pocket to keep them warm because he knew that my mother had a clucking hen. She (the hen) hatched the four eggs but one chick died accidentally when quite young. The other three foraged and flourished on the croft and when they grew large enough to be able to fly they had one wing clipped to prevent them from doing so. They used to stroll down the croft and have a swim in Loch Erisort, but they always came back for lunch!

Just before Christmas, the three were killed and my mother plucked and dressed them. One was to go to an uncle who was Headmaster of Contin School, one to my aunt in Glasgow who had given me the rubber football and the third was to be our own Christmas dinner.

I happened to be in the kitchen when my mother was cleaning the geese and she called to my father: "Roddy, come and see this!" He came, and there beside the sink was an array of rusty screw-nails that she had extracted from the gizzards of the geese. My father turned pale when I looked at him but I said nothing. He had the grace to say: "Tha mi duilich, Iain". (I am sorry, John). The incident shows the danger of relying on circumstantial evidence alone when arriving at a verdict and I always tried to remember it during my years as a schoolteacher.

When I was five years of age the law decreed that I should attend school and my parents were a little worried how I could cope or if I could cope because the system of education in Balallan then was English orientated and my knowledge of English was very limited – in toto, 'Yes' and 'No'.

Prior to my registration my parents tried to prepare me for the inevitable. They used to say to me that when the teacher would ask me my name I would not say 'Iain Ruairidh Sheonaidh' but John Morrison Macleod, my official appellation. This was rehearsed for a couple of weeks before the great day arrived, but I could not understand why my simple name indicating who my father and grandfather were should be changed into incomprehensible jargon! This was further complicated by my memory of a visit to Airidhbhruaich, my mother's birthplace, when I was sent to the shop – Buth Choinnich Bhàin – for a quarter pound of tea – the staple drink in Airidhbhruaich in those days. There were a few ladies present in the shop and one of them asked: "Cò leis a tha am balach?" – (Whose boy is this?) and another answered, "Tha le Ciorstaidh Iain an Tàilleir" – (He is the son of Chrissie, daughter of John, the son of the Tailor) My hackles rose and in as loud a voice as I could muster, I protested, "Chan ann ach le Rodaidh Sheonaidh Amhlaidh" – (No, I belong to Roderick, the son of John, the son of Aulay). This was my male patronymic! It seems I became a male chauvinist at an early age!

However, having been admitted to Balallan School I was placed under the command of the Infant Teacher, whom I regarded as a true Amazon, although she was known as Anna Bheag Choinnich Thormoid – (Little Annie the daughter of Kenneth, the son of Norman) – Miss Mackinnon, Halfway House, Balallan. She must have been a long suffering and patient lady to bear with me and with others through the transitional period of transforming us from being monolingual to being bilingual pupils. She must have managed somehow as I was eventually able to understand the foreign language to a certain degree!

I remember one of my early arithmetic lessons when she said: "If I had a box with six eggs in it and I took four out and put them on the table here and then put one back in the box, how many eggs would be on the table?" I knew the answer but I could not give it to her, because my feeble intellect was thinking – "Why should a clever teacher do a daft thing like that?" Why not take three out of the box in the first place, and there would be three on the table and three in the box? It would have saved her a lot of work as well!

Having acquired an elementary attainment in numeracy I had also progressed to a limited degree in literacy. On one occasion I remember the class being asked to write a story on the subject: "What I would do with my last sixpence". This topic immediately brought to my mind longevity or the lack of it, and being in a somewhat morose mood due to having had a bad day, my story was short and succinct and went thus: "I would buy clothes for my coffin with my last sixpence". I did not know the word 'shroud' at this stage!

On Friday afternoons we were allowed to peruse a bookcase full of books supplied by Coats of Paisley to all schools in Lewis as far as I know and spend the last half hour of the day reading a book. We thought this was a great privilege, but it was not until I became a teacher myself that I realised that this was just a ploy to keep us quiet while the teacher compiled the weekly registration returns! One day I picked up a book called 'Jack and the Beanstalk' and I became so engrossed that at the end of the day I put it back in the middle of the bottom shelf in the hope that no-one would take it before I got to it the following Friday. The ruse worked and it continued to work until I had finished 'Jack and the Beanstalk'.

Having got rid of the imaginary eggs and the shroud I moved into the higher echelons of education in Balallan School, that is the Rum Mòr – the Big Room in every sense of the word. Most of the pupils were bigger than I was and the Headmaster, John Macarthur, stood 6ft 4ins above floor level, almost as high as Roineval, the hill that overlooks Balallan, from my point of view. He had served in World War One, was reputed to have been a piper and he certainly called the tune in the Rum Mòr! His teaching aid was a vicious looking monster which originally had three tentacles but had only two when I first encountered it. Some brave predecessor of mine must have grasped the middle tentacle at the moment of impact and wrenched it off. I have perused the School Log Book of the time but there is no mention of the hero who was responsible for this act of bravery and humanitarianism. His action meant that henceforth a third less surface area of leather would make contact with human flesh. People today get the OBE for less!

Despite Mr Macarthur's failings which were mainly due to his friendship with John Barleycorn he could instil a great deal of Mathematical and English knowledge into the thickest of skulls, and those two subjects were the main two in the curriculum. Pupils leaving Balallan School for The Nicolson Institute learned little new in either subject for the first two years.

When the time came for me to sit my Bursary Examination for entry into The Nicolson Institute, I was in part-time employment filling bobbins for Doilidh a' Bhèiceir, 52 Balallan at a handsome wage of half a crown per tweed and Doilidh could turn out at least two tweeds per week. This was real opulence for me and when the Headmaster asked those who wished to sit the Bursary Examination to put up their hands, I just stared out through the window!

John Macarthur had a flair for repairing wireless sets which were few and far between in the village at that time. However, my father possessed one which had been donated to him by my Uncle Murdo who was then the Church of Scotland minister in Kilmuir, Skye. I still remember that it was a Philips model operated by a dry battery in its stomach and an accumulator, which contained acid, like a car battery, was attached to its umbilical cord. Two accumulators were required because one had to go to Stornoway periodically to be recharged which would take a couple of days and then the standby one would ensure uninterrupted reception.

It was in the month of February that application forms for the Bursary had to be submitted to Dingwall and, as Fate decreed, our wireless broke down in February 1937. My father sent a note to John Macarthur asking if he would call in and have a look at it. This he did one evening and he quickly fixed the wireless. In the ensuing conversation, the Headmaster asked my father why I was not going to sit the Bursary Examination. My father's response was that he had not heard a thing about the Bursary Examination. My younger sister Sophie was in the house and she was sent to my place of work with the message that I was to report home immediately. This I did and I was sent to Airidhbhruaich to ask Miss Maclennan, the Head Teacher there, if she had any blank Application forms left as Mr Macarthur had already sent the Bursary Application forms together with the blank forms to Dingwall.

My father's bicycle was a green Elswick, bought from John Campbell who worked in Eishken, but it had only one rubber handgrip on the handlebars which were chromium plated and shining. It was a cold moonlight night with a few clouds in the sky and I had not gone far when there was a flash of lightning. My mother always put a cloth over the mirrors when there was lightning so I put one hand in my pocket and made for Airidhbhruaich! I got a blank form from Miss Maclennan and got the Bursary!

Brutus said:

"There is a tide in the affairs of men,

Which, taken at the flood, leads to fortune;

Omitted, all the voyages of their life

Is bound in shallows and miseries"

I just caught the flood-tide, but where did the fortune go?!

Before I leave Balallan School, let me recount some of the pastimes my co-ages and I devised for ourselves. The bicycle was the most advanced form of transport available to the proletariat, much faster than the horse and cart and faster even than the horse and gig. The gig was a Rolls Royce model of a cart with springs, originally with steel rimmed wheels but later with solid rubber ones. A new bicycle could be purchased for £4:19:6d (four pounds nineteen shillings and sixpence which is around £250 today after decades of inflation). This sum represented slightly more than a fortnight's wages for the working man and therefore the arrival of a new bicycle in the village was an event worthy of note. The most common makes and models that I can remember were Raleigh, Rudge, B.S.A., Sunbeam and Elswick and many an argument took place regarding the virtues or shortcomings of each model. When a new bicycle was bought the old one, if there was one, was stripped almost bare – wheels, saddle, rubber pedals, chain, brakes, etc., in fact any part that could be utilised for the new bicycle when it began to show signs of wear and tear – the concept of trading-in had still not reached our shores.

It was from the skeletons thus discarded that we boys built our own 'models' and learnt to ride them. A hessian sack would be rolled round the seat pillar and tied with string to serve as a saddle and as long as we could find two wheels, usually tyre-less ones, we had a working machine. There was no need for a chain or free-wheel, and brakes were superfluous. Propulsion was by force of gravity and there were plenty of slopes in Balallan. The only bug-bear was that the local policeman, Sammy Matheson from Skye, had an obsession about lights on bicycles at night.

He stayed at 27 Balallan and used to carry out a foot patrol to the West End at regular intervals, but usually at night. He made a personal local by-law that we must not walk our 'bicycles' along the road at night without lights. How now could we get them to the speed track and back home again? Having been caught on more than one occasion breaking 'Sammy's law' a few of us were on our final warning.

We very much resented this 'law' as usually there was plenty lunar lighting from above: and free lighting at that! Something had to be done and so we convened a St Kilda Parliament. After much discussion and as there was no Speaker to keep us in order some un-Parliamentary language was used when Sammy's name was mentioned! However, the late Ronnie Morrison, 41A Balallan came up with the brilliant suggestion that henceforth when we saw Sammy approaching we should carry the bikes on our shoulders as we went along the road. Had we found a loop-hole in 'Sammy's Law'? At our first encounter with him, with our bicycles on our shoulders we walked in single file to meet him. He stood at the edge of the road, as one did in those days if a funeral procession was passing by. He spoke not a word as we bore our 'bikes' homewards 'by the moonbeams struggling light'. In our hearts we felt that he admired our ingenuity although he did not salute our procession! Sammy's Law was repealed that night!

At a very young age I caught a fever from which I never recovered and never wish to recover – the fishing fever! One evening my father took me to Loch Cuthaig about half a mile behind our home in accordance with the adage – moch gu abhainn is anmoch gu loch – (early to a river and late to a loch). With his bamboo rod and worms as bait he caught a beautiful brown trout which I was allowed to carry home. On the way I examined it thoroughly, noting the beautiful colouring from the dark back, green body and golden underside. The large dark spots all over its body except on the underside were intermingled with small red ones near the tail. Now and again I would hold the fish to my nose and smell it and I am sure it was that fragrant aroma that caused my life-long fever!

In the spring of 1937 an epidemic of whooping cough was raging in Stornoway and a Balallan pupil in The Nicolson Institute brought it to Balallan. It was a very virulent strain and some youngsters suffered greatly. I remember my father carrying my younger sister Sophia outside because her face had turned blue due to the whooping. My wife Margaret remembers a similar occurrence happened to her sister Iana.

I did not suffer badly and by early summer I was left at home with my grandfather while my mother and father went to the Eishken road to work at our peats. It was assumed that I would stay at home and look after my grandfather but as I had thought that I had completely recovered from the whooping cough I became susceptible to the fever I had caught some years before, and so I searched for and found an empty cocoa tin which I cleaned. Then I collected some worms and having checked that my grandfather was hale and hearty, I took my father's bamboo rod, tied it to the crossbar of his Elswick bicycle and sallied forth to the Abhainn Mhòr at the west end of the village. That river flows from Loch Stranndavat and it had a run of salmon at that time. In fact, Lady d'Oyly Carte, the then proprietrix of Soval Estate, used to fish it quite often with her gillie, John Macleod, 70 Balallan.

In the meantime, the chauffeur of her Rolls Royce had to while away his time during their absence at the loch – he must have been a very enterprising individual because he devised a method of catching fish, preparing and eating them al fresco if the weather was favourable. Fishmongers often travelled from Lewis to Harris in vans and on their return they used to wash the empty fish boxes in a small pool just above the bridge on the Abhainn Mhòr. Naturally, scraps of fish were deposited and this attracted eels. The eels attracted the chauffeur who used to catch them probably with line, hook and worm. Among his culinary equipment he had a metal tripod and a flexible piece of wire with which he attached the cleaned eel to the tripod.

In bygone days, peat used to be cut in the vicinity and stacked by the roadside prior to carting them home. In those stances there was plenty of peat dross and fragments of black peat (caoran dubh). A fire of peat and heather, of which there was no dearth in Eilean an Fhraoich, would then be lit and the smoke and heat expertly directed to the suspended eel. The result would be a mouth watering and delicious snack for the English chauffeur but in those days it would be an anathema to a Lewisman, many of whom believed that freshwater eels originated from the hair of a dog! Even some Lewismen who had been lifelong fishermen would not allow a conger eel to be brought into their homes. They had been used to seeing roes in all other fish except the conger and thus a false conception was created as they had never heard of the Sargasso Sea!

But I digress; I was on my way to fish the large round pool on the Abhainn

Mhòr about fifty yards above the bridge. Soon after arriving there I hauled a silvery salmon on to the bank, but the excitement brought on a bout of the whooping cough and in order to stop the salmon from slipping back into the pool, I sat on it. In the meantime, a tinker lad about my own age whose family had a tent near the bridge came along and started demanding the salmon. This revived me and I killed the salmon in my own way – I did not have a priest! (A priest is a piece of wood with a loop at the end to put round the wrist. It is used to kill the fish in a humane way by hitting it over the head). Then I threatened to throw my tormentor into the pool unless he made for his tent immediately. He complied, possibly because he had never seen anybody sitting on a salmon whooping and vomiting and there again, he may have been a non-swimmer!

When I arrived home with my prize I showed it proudly to my grandfather whose response when he examined it was: "Go and throw it in the midden!"

"Why?" I asked him, completely shocked. He told me it was a kelt (a salmon in deteriorating condition after spawning) and gave me a lesson on how to recognise a kelt from a freshly run fish. I never forgot the lesson and many a kelt owed its life to this in later years!

When I was eight years of age I could not swim and on one cold November evening when I was fishing for cuddies on Creag Martainn in Loch Erisort I fell head first into the sea when the stone I was standing on toppled over. Two factors saved my life:

1) that I was wearing a heavy tweed coat which acted as a life jacket before it became waterlogged and

2) that it was half-tide and I was able to drag myself ashore by pulling at the seaweed at a furious speed.

The following summer I decided to learn to swim! This I did without any tuition and alone because swimming trunks were not in vogue in Balallan in the thirties and I was a shy boy! I was thankful a decade later that I had learnt the rudiments of survival in the water because the RAF in Arbroath had a very basic way of teaching recruits to swim. The squad was lined up along the side of the swimming pool and the front line was ordered to jump in. Anyone who had the temerity to inform the corporal in charge that he could not swim was given a hefty push into the pool – within a week all the squad could swim!

This method of teaching swimming is reminiscent of a similar method practised in Balallan at one time. The late Donald Mackenzie (Dòmhnall Luis), 28 Balallan used to tell me that he got swimming tuition from Roderick Macleod (Rodaidh Sheonaidh), 25 Balallan. Roddy who was a strong swimmer, used to take Donald on his shoulders, swim out a fair distance from the shore and then dive, leaving poor Donald floundering in the water. Roddy would surface and escort and advise Donald as he splashed his way shorewards; Donald became a competent swimmer in a short time! During World War 1, Roddy and Donald Macdonald (Dòmhchan), 14 Balallan served in the Navy but on different ships which at one time were anchored some distance apart in the Adriatic and Roddy who had not seen Dòmhchan for some time just swam across for a 'cèilidh'.

In the winter apart from cycling, the next favourite pastime was sliding on the road during frosty weather. The usual venue was from the school gate downhill to Halfway House at Allt Bun an Ard, and the criterion aimed at for a perfect slide was 'gum biodh am botal-dubh oirre', ie that it would be shining black. The winter tackety boots were excellent skates!

Also in winter there was an opportunity to earn a few coppers by collecting whelks at the ebb of the Spring tides (reodhart), but unfortunately this did not always occur on Saturdays. On one occasion when Ronnie Morrison, 41 Balallan and I had dodged school (chan fhuirich muir ri uallach is cha bhuain cas luath maorach – the tide will not wait for one who worries and a fast-footed person will not collect shellfish) we were on our way with a sackful of whelks in a barrow to market – Bùth a' Cheannaich at 20 Balallan (the local shop). For obvious reasons we travelled at night as our route passed by the school but as luck would have it we met the Headmaster John Macarthur halfway up the hill and as a full moon was shining mutual recognition was inevitable. We stopped – whether through shock or exhaustion I am not sure. He greeted us with a question as usual enquiring what we had in the barrow. We told him and he asked if he could have a few. We were only too glad to comply and we filled his pockets, not through generosity but as a 'sop to Cerberus'! Next day he did not even ask us why we had been absent the previous day – he must have enjoyed the whelks! The measure Coinneach a' Cheannaich used was a large bucket (ciorda) and the going price was 2s 6d per bucket – not a fortune but something to ease our penury.

It did not matter what season of the year it was we youngsters in Balallan found ways of passing the time and entertaining ourselves. There is a Scots adage: 'never cast a cloot until May is oot' – but we always cast our boots long before 'Latha Buidhe Bealltuinn' simply because there was not much left of the old ones by then! At first, going barefoot was not very pleasant due to the softness of our soles, but it did not take long for them to harden despite being mollycoddled in tackety boots over the winter months.

My boyhood friend was Roderick John Mackenzie (Iain Shuarnaidh, 54 Balallan) who was tragically killed in a road accident after the War, in which he had undergone active service in the Army. He and I used to carry out our first test of endurance by running across an area of moorland that had been burnt (falasgair) during the Spring. Although the pain was excruciating it would be 'infra dig' to hesitate on that journey of self-inflicted torture. Thereafter, having extracted charred bits of heather from the soles of our feet, we found no problem in running along 'metalled' roads or any other rough terrain. The Litter Act had not been thought of but it was the custom that everyone, young and old, would pick up any fragments of glass, or any other article that could cause injury and place them between the stones in a wall, out of harm's way.

Nowadays when the trout fishing season begins the wind blows from the north and persists from that direction for most of the season. In the thirties it invariably blew from the south or south west with balmy days in May and June when the trout were voraciously hungry and delighted in a meal of red luscious juicy worms presented with expertise by the angler with his 14ft bamboo rod.

When Iain and I set off fishing we would carry an empty cocoa tin and by turning over oldish cowpats we could fill the tin before we reached Loch Cuthaig. Today, worms are difficult, if not impossible to find on the moorland because there are few cows in the area, and hence fewer cowpats

The modern trend is to go to a Fishing Tackle shop where a small plastic tub of fifteen worms, which I believe come from Norway, can be purchased for about £1.35. Should we have had such a market, we could have become 'worm millionaires' in a season!

During our wanderings on the moor, if we spotted a bee buzzing around, we would try to follow it to the hive – Iain was an expert at this – and pulling our 'gensies' over our heads we would extract a comb, devour half of the honey and replace the honeycomb. This would not be too catastrophic for the bees who could, by working overtime, replenish their loss.

Balallan in the old days – looking towards Harris over the school and the area where the Lochs Agricultural Show is now held every year

Chapter 2

White Horse to the Rescue

In those days there were two hostels in Stornoway, the Louis Carnegie Girls' Hostel and the Elizabeth Haldane Boys' Hostel, which were meant to accommodate pupils from the rural areas who lived beyond commuting distance from Stornoway. However, with the large influx of pupils from the 'country' to The Nicolson Institute there was not sufficient accommodation to house them all in the hostels so lodgings or 'digs', as they were known had to be found for the surplus. I started off in Maciver Buildings, an off-shoot of Keith Street, but they have long since disappeared. My co-lodgers were the late Angus Campbell from Bragar, Calum Macleod from Shawbost and Alex Dan Macleod from Garyvard. Our landlady was Bean Chalum 'an Phortair and her husband who belonged to Point. She was a very kind, patient and tolerant person. He was equally kind but not quite as patient or tolerant and if we misbehaved he was not averse to giving us a cuff in the ear; after all, he was in 'loco parentis'. We accepted our chastisement with bonhomie and we never objected as we knew we deserved it.

The usual arrangement in 'digs' was that we would bring in all the food we required and the landlady would cook it and serve it and also decide what the menu for each day would be. On the occasion when meat was selected we all had our different favourite cuts which were put into a large pot and boiled to make soup. In order to recognise who owned each cut of meat, three of us were allocated three different coloured pieces of string which were tied round our individual meat contributions, the owner of the meat with no string was known to her and I remember that we never questioned her sense of colour! We were also provided with a bed between two and for those services and many others each of us was charged six shillings or 30p per week in today's currency.

Parochialism must have been rampant because the Siarachs shared one bed and the Lochies the other! The Siarach Calum was a hefty lad. It is said that the first solid food that Calum partook of in his infancy was 'biorach air a chlobha' (dogfish roasted on tongs) and so there is little wonder that he was such a stalwart adolescent and is still a fit and stalwart octogenarian! However, Alex Dan used to torment him on a Sunday morning by firing cardboard missiles from a catapult across the room and aimed at Calum's backside as he lay in bed. Even in those days, Calum was a strict Sabbath observer as he still is and he would take no action except to inform Alex Dan sternly that Diluain a' Bhreabain (the day of retribution) was nigh! It is not long since Calum reminded

The Francis Street building of The Nicolson Institute ... now Museum nan Eilean

me that I used to act as referee in the Monday morning battles!

I had an account with John Smith, Butcher (Seonaidh a Bhragaidh) who had a shop on the corner of Church Street and Keith Street, and another one with A & J Martin, North Beach (Ailean and Seonaidh Barabal) for my groceries. A & J Martin belonged to Airidhbhruaich, my mother's birthplace and that is probably why they were favoured with my custom! Payment was made at the end of each term – there were three in the school year – and as the annual bursary was £27 we had £9 to meet our termly budget – there was never any surplus but always a deficit!

I still had the 'shining morning face' and the satchel but I was no longer 'creeping like a snail unwillingly to school'. This was a great adventure finding my way to school through the metropolis, entering the imposing Francis Street building, sitting in awe in a classroom with thirty nine others and wondering how the world could hold so many people.

In 1937 I was in Class 1A on the ground floor – in the room with three windows to the right; 1B was to the left. Our class teacher was Miss Ina

Macdonald who was always calm and collected and elegantly attired. Two years later Margaret MacIver, who became my wife started off her secondary education in the same classroom and she still follows me around!

On second year I moved upstairs to Class 2A where the teacher was Kenneth Mackenzie who belonged to the West Coast of Scotland and was a veteran of World War One. He always wore his trousers at half-mast and was unmarried. Although he never suffered fools gladly I was very fond of him as a teacher. His main teaching subject was Mathematics but he also taught Science. On one occasion at a science lesson the experiment was to make distilled water by heating ordinary water until steam was produced and then cooling that steam until it re-liquefied. When the distilled water thus formed was collected in a beaker he showed it to a girl from Uig and asked her what was in the beaker, "Water" she replied. "What water? Your Granny's water?" he retorted in exasperation! After all, he had gone to a lot of trouble to produce *distilled* water!

We soon got used to the school routine – 9am opening, 4.15pm closing, with eight periods in between; double periods for practical subjects and single periods for the rest. The day soon passed because of the variety of the subjects and the variety of teachers, which was so unlike primary school.

The Rector, John Macrae, was a small man, but 'chan e a bhith beag a bhith bog', (to be small is not to be soft) and he was a hard task master. He taught mathematics to the higher classes and I had him on Class VI. I can honestly say that he was the best Maths teacher I ever came across. He could explain abstruse mathematical concepts with such clarity and simplicity that few could fail to understand him. He used to play in the School football team when he was younger as did other teachers such as Trail, Chalmers, Nicol and Kenny Mackenzie. The 1938 team, which I can still rattle off, cleared the boards, and we younger pupils idolised the players and wished to emulate them – there were no teachers in that team! A story circulating in the school and based on Johnnie 'Craes' football skill was probably apocryphal. It claimed that on one occasion when he was teaching Maths in Class VI room, the chalk broke as he was writing on the board and that he deftly kicked the broken piece through the open window before it could reach the floor!

Unfortunately with the outbreak of war organised football in Lewis came to a standstill and the best we could hope for was to organise a team amongst ourselves and challenge a team from any naval ship that happened to visit Stornoway; some of those games were hilarious!

In my second year at The Nicolson I acquired a second hand Post Office bicycle and I cycled home most weekends. I happened to be home when the Second World War was declared – Sunday 3 September 1939. The day was wet and stormy and I postponed my return until Monday morning – I used to travel back on Sunday evenings. There was a very strong southerly wind on Monday morning and I made the journey in record time, but when I arrived at The Nicolson the place was practically deserted. Apparently on Sunday evening it had been announced in all the churches in Stornoway that The Nicolson would be closed for a week, but because of poor communications at the time word had not percolated to Balallan or to many other villages in the hinterland of Lewis. The first pupil I met was Neily Neily from Point and he said: "Well John, the Germans have got first blood – the Athenia was sunk off Lewis last night." Little did I know at the time that a fellow pupil from Balallan school, Sydney Evans, was aboard as a crew member. The Athenia was a passenger ship bound for America and although there was heavy loss of life, fortunately Sydney survived and was later awarded the Royal Humane Society Bronze Medal following German bombing of shipping in the Thames. The war cast a gloom over the whole school especially when news came of the death of some ex-pupil we knew.

At the beginning of 1942 while I was still a pupil at the Nicolson, the Lewis Squadron of the Air Training Corps (ATC) was formed – No 1731 Squadron – and this number was carried on the shoulders of our uniform jackets. I was a founder member as was John Murray from North Tolsta and as far as I know we are the only surviving founder members now (2008) in Lewis but there may be others elsewhere.

We used to attend lectures in The Nicolson Institute conducted mainly by RAF members then stationed at Stornoway but we also had a first class Instructor in the person of Mr Duncan Macdonald, then teaching Commercial Subjects in the Nicolson. The RAF personnel taught us Aircraft Identification, sending and receiving messages by Morse Code and "square-bashing" amongst other things.

Under the supervision of Mr Macdonald we acquired the engine of a Lanchester car put out to grass by the late Dr Doig, the Medical Officer of Health. The car was located at Goathill Crescent and the engine was removed and placed in a wheelbarrow which was not an easy task. It was no easier to trundle the barrow to the Technical Department of The Nicolson Institute but with two sturdy lads at each handle it was done – mechanical transport and petrol were both in short supply.

The engine was set up on a work bench and Mr Macdonald showed us how to dismantle it bit by bit, clean the parts and set them aside. He also explained to us the function of each part and soon the engine was a mere skeleton. Then the operation to put Humpty Dumpty back together again commenced and soon the now gleaming bits and pieces were replaced and there were no leftovers – a good omen!

The basic essentials required to start an engine are (1) fuel and (2) a spark to ignite the fuel. Mr Macdonald devised a fuel-tank from ingenious adaptations to a biscuit box and ignition was provided by a brawny arm on the starting handle. A loud cheer rent the atmosphere together with a cloud of blue smoke as the engine burst into life! Why should Britain tremble!

In August 1942 the ATC set off to Alness where we were billeted in bell-tents. On arrival I had a raging headache and reported to the Orderly Officer. He sent me to an isolation tent which had the luxury of a wooden floor and a palliasse but was crawling with earwigs! The only visitor I had that evening was the late Kenny Murdo Maciver, 3 Laxay who brought me a newspaper – very thoughtful! The rest of my mates must have thought I had the plague but in the morning when I went to Sick Quarters it transpired I had just a size 10 cold! After Kenny Murdo left I slaughtered as many of the earwigs as I could but after a while I realised I was engaged in a losing battle and gave up. I stuffed my ears with bits of Kenny Murdo's paper and got my head down forgetting all the gruesome stories I had heard about those horrible creatures entering people's brain via the ears!

The camp was attended by A.T.C. Squadrons from all over the Highlands including Aviemore and the commander-in-chief was Cameron of Locheil who paid us a visit at lunch-time one day in the marquee where we were dining. All the Squadrons had different numbers emblazoned on their shoulder flashes. Cameron prided himself in being able to identify all cadet Squadrons from the number on their shoulders and as he walked round the marquee he stopped behind a cadet, looked at his number, tapped him on the shoulder and said "Aviemore?". The lad turned round and innocently replied, "No thank you, Sir. I've had enough!"

The highlight of our training trip was to be a flight in a Sunderland Flying Boat to which we all looked forward very much. At that time the main base for Sunderlands was Oban but some were also based at Invergordon. My turn came on the 25th August 1942 and our group were marching along the pier at Invergordon with a RAF NCO in charge and we were proudly wearing our Mae Wests (lifejackets named after a famous film star for obvious reasons!). Suddenly a Dispatch Rider roared alongside, stopped his motor-bike beside the NCO and handed him a paper. The NCO called the squad to a halt, read the paper and then gave the command: "About turn, quick march".

We were absolutely bewildered and when we arrived back at base we questioned the NCO but we received no enlightenment.

It was later that we learned that not long before our "About turn"the Duke of Kent and his entourage had been picked up at Invergordon by a Sunderland from Oban and on their way to Iceland had crashed near Dunbeath in Caithness in mysterious circumstances: the only survivor was Andrew Jack, the rear gunner. A veil was placed over the whole affair and even in post-war years few specific details concerning the tragic accident were published.

On our return to Lewis from the camp some of us, and I was included, had to face the task of studying for our Highers which we would sit the following March. With the certainty that we would be called up as soon as we sat them and with the uncertainty of our futures, it was sometimes difficult to concentrate 100% on our studies. However, by casting aside any pessimistic thoughts that the Devil presented to me I was able to carry on studying to the best of my ability and was successful in obtaining a group of subjects at Higher grade that would make me eligible for entry to University.

However, on my last Friday in school I was sitting Higher Mathematics and I started seeing black spots on my examination paper. I plodded on, resting now and again until the black spots disappeared. At that time measles were raging in The Nicolson and I was sure I had contracted them.

I made for home in Balallan as soon as school was dismissed hitching a lift on a workmen's bus – the workmen being local men working at the aerodrome in Stornoway. As soon as the bus set off most of the occupants lit up their pipes and a cloud of Black Twist tobacco soon pervaded the atmosphere. It was not long before the temperature in the bus rose and brought out my measles rash. A neighbour, John Nicolson, 45 Balallan sitting next to me in the bus exclaimed in Gaelic: "John, what on earth is wrong with your face?"

"Just pimples, John," I replied. In those days people were very afraid of measles and with good reason. I was afraid if I admitted what I feared was the truth I would be thrown off the bus! It was a "mad March day" and as soon as I stepped off the bus and the fierce, cold east wind hit me the rash must have disappeared. When I got inside our home my mother knew that something was wrong with me and I told her I thought I had measles. She went to consult our next door neighbour having asked me to go to bed. Our neighbour was Donald Macmillan a noted meteorologist, a useful amateur vet and he was also the local postman. I was not sure which, if any, of those qualifications would succour me in my hour of need but I had no need to worry. He arrived with an unopened bottle of White Horse whisky, climbed the stairs to my bedroom, followed by my mother, had one look at me, put his hand on my brow and then ordered my mother to bring a tumbler and a kettle of hot water. When this arrived he half filled the tumbler with whisky, topped it up with hot water and ordered in Gaelic: "Ol siud!" (Drink that!)

The time was approximately 6.30pm on Friday and when I woke on Sunday morning my measles rash had reappeared and I felt fine!

Ever since then whenever I see a white horse in a field or on the moor or anywhere else, my mind goes back to the excellent "medical practitioner" who may have saved my life when I took measles. When I was "demobbed" after World War Two, I always used to call on him at New Year and gave him a good tot of White Horse – he lived until he was 95!

Chapter 3

Off to War and a Breakfast of Kippers at Mallaig

Very shortly after I recovered from the measles I received a communication from the RAF headquarters ordering me to report to an address in Edinburgh at 9am on 12th April 1943 and to bring with me an empty case in which my civilian clothes would be returned home. A travel warrant was enclosed but there were no instructions regarding the route nor any mention of a reception party to meet me!

I made my way to Stornoway, 15 miles from my home and on the 10th of April I boarded the "Lochness" after midnight to sail across a turbulent Minch to disembark at Kyle of Lochalsh. The journey took about five hours but as I never suffered from "mal de mer" I just got my head down in a quiet corner. The train journey from Kyle was very uncomfortable because of crowded carriages but I eventually arrived at Princes St Station about 11 pm. There I met a lad who was joining the Bevin Boys (young men conscripted to work in the coal mines) and we chatted until his train came in about 2am.

Then I got my head down again on a hard station bench and set the alarm device incorporated somewhere in my system for 8.30 am. It worked. I got to my specified destination somehow – I had never been in Edinburgh before – and found about 100 other recruits milling around. We were ushered into a large hall which contained tables and benches. The RAF Sergeant in charge told us we were going to sit an Aptitude Test and handed each of us a Test Paper. There was no word as yet of anything to eat but perhaps the powers-that-be thought that one is more intelligent on an empty stomach!

After the time allowed for the test the papers were taken away and corrected by an anonymous team whom we never saw and in due course they were handed back to us. To my surprise I did remarkably well!

I cannot remember much after the test until I found myself on a train with many others heading for Arbroath. When we arrived there we formed a long queue outside the Stores through which we passed slowly while a WAAF behind each stall would give us a cursory glance and threw to us whichever item of uniform she was dispensing. The only question I remember being asked was what size my shoes were. When we got back to our "billets", which were a derelict mill baptised Stalingrad by previous inmates after the Russian city reduced to rubble during the German offensive, I discovered that I had been issued with two left gumboots (RAF name for Wellington boots) and when I went back with them to the Stores the WAAF Sergeant in charge refused to replace them.

However, my guardian angel was looking after me! The officer in charge of equipment at Arbroath at that time was Flight Lieutenant Murdo Macleod from Habost, Lochs, married to Mary Macdonald of 52 Balallan and I lived at No. 50. When our civilian clothes were being sent home a list of the names and addresses was made which was passed on to the Equipment Officer who examined it. When he saw my name and address he sent for me and invited me to a meal the next Sunday. He and his family were living in a private residence in Arbroath. During the course of the evening Murdo asked me how I was getting on in the RAF. I told him that I was enjoying everything except my gumboots and I told him the whole story. He was infuriated and asked me to tell the NCO in charge of my squad that I had an appointment with him on Thursday morning and he also told me to bring my gum-boots along when I came to the office at 10 o'clock. The Sgt WAAF would be at the counter and he would be in the inner office and so he told me to speak out loudly when I was addressing her. This I did and the WAAF Sergeant did likewise when a sprog airman dared to address her as I did! Murdo soon appeared and demanded to know "What's going on here?" I promptly stood to attention, saluted and explained my complaint. "Airman, stand at ease" said the Flight Lieutenant and then laid into the Sergeant accusing her of incompetence, dereliction of duty and bringing the Service into disrepute. He asked me to hand her my gumboots while she shed copious amount of tears of, I hope, remorse but more likely of resentment. As Murdo stormed back into his office, I stood to attention and gave him another salute. He deserved it!

Life in Arbroath was pretty strenuous but being young and fit, I relished it. A few years ago Margaret, my wife and I visited Arbroath on our way south and I took her to visit the salt water swimming pool. Unfortunately it had closed the previous week but we could see in through a window. Memories flooded back of the days in 1943 when we used to be marched daily to the pool and lined up on one side of it. Then came the order "Front line jump in". Some would say "I can't swim Corporal". "Can't you?" the Corporal would reply as he pushed the protestor into the pool! There were always two lifeguards around the pool to haul out anyone who was in serious difficulties but at the end of a week everyone in the squad was able to swim!

After leaving Arbroath I went to RAF Halton not far from London to train as a mechanic. This was perhaps the RAF's biggest and best training centre and I found the Instructors excellent and meticulous. For example when we were given the task to cut a square say of 2" from a piece of mild steel about half an inch thick we took the finished article to the Instructor who measured it with his micrometer – the tolerance of error was three thou (three thousandths of an inch). If he passed our effort we then had to drill and shape a square in a block of similar steel into which our square would fit with the same tolerance. It is no wonder that we spent about a fortnight drilling and filing but it taught us the importance of precision in our future handling of any mechanical process that we undertook; I find that after over 60 years the training still rubs off on me.

The engine that we trained on at Halton was a Rolls Royce Merlin – a wonderful piece of engineering. This model had all its moving parts exposed by skilful cutting and were painted red. This enabled us to understand and appreciate the different functions of all the most important parts in this masterpiece.

When we had successfully finished our course at Halton we were posted to various RAF stations in order to gain experience in dealing with a variety of aero-engines both British and American. Among the stations I served on was Thornaby-on-Tees. When stationed there, I met a chap Gordon Shepherd from Bishop Auckland and we became pals. One day when we were off duty we went to Durham and as we were walking along a street Gordon shouted "There's my girlfriend and her mother!" and off we went to catch up with them. I followed at a slower pace and Gordon introduced me to Joyce and her mother Mrs Bagnall. Needless to say Gordon and Joyce paired off and Mrs Bagnall and I followed on behind. Eventually we went into a café for tea or coffee and Mrs Bagnall who lived in a small mining village not very far away called Roddymoor gave me her address and asked me to call there should I ever be passing that way. As Gordon and I were pending posting overseas it did not seem likely that I would ever visit Roddymoor – however, on New Year's Eve 1946 I did end up at Roddymoor having landed at Northolt airfield from Egypt the previous day, but more about that later on.

The only Islesman I came across while serving in the UK was John Smith whose people ran the South Boisdale Post Office at that time. We met at Brackley and as John was a Gaelic speaker we immediately became friends. The Station Warrant Officer was actually based in the Admin Dept but occasionally he came into the hangar where we were working to check that there was no skylarking taking place. John and I always spoke Gaelic to each other as we worked and as soon as the S.W.O. appeared we would raise our voices and laugh loudly as if we were enjoying some joke. Naturally, the S.W.O. would think that we were laughing at him and he was not far wrong, but he could do nothing about it except take a huge dislike to us both.

When the time came for me to apply for leave, a Welsh airman who apparently knew me although I did not know him approached me and asked me if I was going on leave to Lewis. I confirmed that I was and then he informed me that according to AMO 1073/42 (Air Ministry Order), I was entitled to spend my whole leave on the Island. This was great news as the normal procedure was to apply for travelling time when going on leave to remote areas.

On arrival at Stornoway pier after midnight I found a box near the end of the gangway occupied by an RAF S.P. (Special Police) man. I asked him to stamp my leave pass, which he did. At that time there was also a small RAF unit temporary hut situated on South Beach esplanade where airmen home on leave could find information and guidance without having to travel to the RAF base about three miles outside Stornoway. Towards the end of my leave I called at the hut and asked to have my leave pass endorsed to the effect that I was due to leave Stornoway by 23.59 on the appropriate date. This was done and I embarked on the 'Loch Ness' before the stipulated time and had my leave pass stamped. The journey across the Minch did not worry me as I never suffered from 'mal de mer'. After a journey south affected by delays I arrived in Brackley where I was immediately put on a charge: AWOL – Absent Without Leave!

As I was escorted into the presence of the 'Procurator Fiscal' as we would call him, my escort pulled off my cap and threw it to the floor! I resented this but as I was on my first charge in the RAF I did not know this was normal procedure! The Judge, or whatever appellation applied to him, who was a Flight Lieutenant read out the charge probably compiled by the S.W.O. who would have had plenty of practice. He then asked me what I had to say. I replied that I pled innocent of being Absent Without Leave because according to AMO 1073/42, I was entitled to spend my whole leave on the Island of Lewis and I had documentation to prove I had done so.

That shook him! Then he told my escort to go and fetch the said AMO, but that individual seemed to get lost. Eventually, the Officer told me to stand at ease and this I did giving the floor a good thump but still I stared at him. When my escort eventually returned with the relevant AMO the Officer read it and probably decided that the only way to get me was to prove that I took an inordinately long time to travel from Stornoway to Brackley. Therefore he asked for a detailed account. This I gave, spending quite a while aboard the 'Loch Ness' which battled bravely across the Minch against the south-west gale. At Kyle I found the train for Inverness had departed hours earlier. The next train I caught was a really slow one and it stopped at Achnaseileach for some time. When it arrived at Achnasheen the lights at the level crossing were not functioning and the train driver quite rightly would not move until the fault was rectified. By the time we got to Achnanallt I was getting worried about accommodation for the night. My inquisitor must have been in quite a daze by this time and he said: "Tell me where you went after leaving Stromness?".

"Sir ," I said, "I was never in Stromness in all my life. Stromness as you know is in the Orkney Isles". He muttered something, looked at the AMO

1073/42 for a few seconds and pronounced the verdict: "Case dismissed!"

When I arrived at the hangar I reported my return to the S.W.O. who was really shocked. He tried to quiz me but I told him I had an urgent job to do and left his office. However, it was not long until he got his revenge. A short time later I ended up in Blackpool awaiting a posting overseas which took me to Egypt. John Smith happened to be home on leave in Uist at this time and he had been given seven days extension of leave from his GP and thus he missed the draft I was on but as soon as he returned to base he was put on another draft and he ended up in Burma.

During one end-of-leave journey south, we stopped in Glasgow where we had a photograph taken in a studio with John wearing full Highland Dress, which could be hired for a pittance in the studio. John was not very tall but he was well built and carried the kilt elegantly. Due to the "exigencies of the Service" as the official jargon put it, we were not able to collect the photographs but we had a receipt proving that we had paid for them and a friend was able to collect them later and send a copy to each of our homes.

This took place in mid-1944 but for me an interesting sequel occurred in January 1951. On a really stormy night with a storm blowing from the North East a fishing boat from Leurbost – the 'True Love' – was making for Stornoway from the Loch Shell area. After rounding Kebbock Head she faced the full force of the storm and before she made it safely to port the propeller shaft sheared. The skipper was the late Murdo Macleod (Murchadh Frìth) from Leurbost and he was a very experienced seaman having had command of a naval ship during the war. When Murdo realised what had happened he and the crew tied a bundle of herring nets together to form a sea anchor which thrown over the bow with a strong rope attached would hold the bow of the 'True Love' into the wind.

Many Lewis students returning from their Christmas holidays to University and College were aboard the 'Loch Seaforth' which had replaced the good old 'Loch Ness'. I was one of those students and Norman Martin, 13 Balallan, a near neighbour and I were standing at the starboard rail fairly far forward when the 'Loch Seaforth' took a violent turn to port which buried most of the starboard rail aft of us under water. When the ship eventually recovered we found ourselves in the port scuppers soaked to the skin! My brother-in-law Rev Norman Macsween who was in a bunk down below found himself standing on the side of the ship – the inside of course!

It transpired that the helmsman had spotted the lights of the 'True Love' ahead and had taken violent avoiding action. There were some minor injuries among the passengers but it was a blessing that no-one was lost overboard. As for the 'True Love', she kept drifting towards the Shiant Isles and when they were dangerously close they threw two anchors overboard which held. In those days fishing boats like the 'True Love' did not carry a radio but the crew lit oily rags which were spotted by the keepers of Glas Island Lighthouse, Scalpay and the Stornoway Lifeboat came to the rescue.

The 'Loch Seaforth' slowed down considerably and when we arrived in Mallaig, the Glasgow train had gone. A large number of passengers went to the West Highland Hotel and as we were not expected the only menu they could offer us was salt herring or kippers! There were not sufficient kippers for everyone so the maids came round asking who would take salt herring. I volunteered, in fact I could have eaten a horse, but when the maid came to serve me, she gave me a kipper and asked if I had ever been in the RAF. When I answered in the affirmitive she asked if I knew a John Smith from South Uist. Again I answered that I did but added that I did not recollect ever seeing her. "You never did see me but do you remember having your photograph taken with my brother John who was wearing the kilt when you were both in the RAF?" Yes I did, but I never thought it would earn me a kipper for breakfast instead of salt herring in Mallaig years afterwards!

Back in mid-1944, I was posted to Blackpool awaiting an unknown ship to carry me to an unknown destination. While at Blackpool four of us were billeted in a private house with nothing to do but spend the little money we had! At last a truck came and took us at night carrying our full kit to Liverpool. At the pier in Liverpool we were lined up and asked to wait until our turn came to embark. To me the 'Alcantara' a troopship of 22,000 tons lying alongside the pier was an awesome sight. A continuous flow of service-men, Navy, Army and Air Force, carrying full kit steadily climbed a fairly steep gangway. It reminded me of the night I stood on the pier in Stornoway as a 15-year-old in 1939 and watched RNR volunteers embarking on the 'Lochness', a toy compared with the 'Alcantara'.

Eventually our detachment got aboard and we were led to E-deck, right down in the bowels of the ship. There we were shown our sleeping quarters which consisted of an open space with hammocks laid out neatly and the wherewithal to hang them above us. To the sailors who embarked it would be no problem to get into a hammock but to the Army and Air Force landlubbers it was a major undertaking! I discovered a pole beside where I was and I decided to sling my hammock beside it as I could climb up the pole and slip into my hammock without any trouble. This worked admirably the first night but when we got into the open sea and the 'Alcantara' began to roll, matters were different. When the ship rolled to starboard the hammocks to port of me also swung to starboard until they made contact with my hammock which stopped the movement when my hammock and I made contact with the pole, to the detriment of my ribs! Of course, the same thing happened when the ship took the opposite roll! I soon abandoned hammock and slept on the floor – or to be more nautical, on the deck!

In Blackpool awaiting posting overseas. I am on the far left.

In our dining room we sat at benches, ten on each side. There was an NCO at the top who dispensed the meals on plates which were passed down to the unfortunates who sat at the far end of the benches, and I was one of them. By giving smaller portions to us he was sure there would be more than ample left in the urn to provide a good meal for himself and his cronies beside him. One day I got annoyed at the meagre portions we at the lower end of the table received and I told my mates not to touch theirs as I was going to lodge a protest when everyone was served. When this was done I took my plate hidden behind my back and walked up to the top of the table.

"Corporal" I said "Are you not supposed to serve the food in equal portions?"

"Of course and that's what I'm doing," he barked.

"OK, Corporal, will you then exchange your plate with mine," I said as I produced it from behind my back.

He flew into a rage but then the Orderly Officer fortuitously appeared and asked what the trouble was. I explained to him and when he saw the difference in the contents of the two plates he said "Corporal, exchange your plate with the airman's." As I arrived at the bottom of the table there were cheers from my neighbours. Next day there was a different NCO serving the food!

Despite the fact that our share of the food at the bottom of the table vastly improved I was still very hungry. There is a Gaelic saying "Balach òg is e ri fàs dh'itheadh e mar mheileadh bràth" (A young growing lad could eat as fast as a quern could grind.) This was very true as far as I was concerned and when we ran into heavy seas a few days into the Atlantic almost all the boys around me turned green and pushed their plates aside. I told them politely that if they did not eat their food it would end up in the swill-bin. They then offered their plates to me and watched me with a mixture of disgust and envy as I cleared about four of them!

Later, I had qualms of conscience and felt somewhat guilty that I had satiated my voracious appetite at the expense of my comrades. However, reason prevailed and salved my conscience by pointing out to me that if I had not partaken of the food it would have been wasted and waste of food in time of war was inexcusable! Fortunately for my conscience and for the welfare of my mates the gale abated in a couple of days and everyone was scraping his plate clean!

Eventually after having sailed west and then south we turned east and so we guessed where we were heading. While we were sailing through rough weather I admired the tenacity of our Naval escorts who when we came on deck in the morning were in exactly the same position as they occupied when we went below the previous evening. Below we were, down on E-deck and should a torpedo strike when we were down there the chances of survival were not very good. It is not surprising therefore that we spent as much time as possible up top!

When we were about two days from Gibraltar a U-boat seems to have been lying in wait for us and the first indication that we had of anything being amiss was when our escorting destroyer ahead of the convoy began throwing depth charges overboard and circling round a certain location. The 'Alcantara' leading the starboard column altered course slightly to starboard and the 'Mauretania' leading the port column altered course slightly to port and left the destroyer room to manoeuvre. Meantime another destroyer came speeding through the convoy and both were dropping depth charges. The explosions sent a shudder through our ship of 22,000 tons and they must have wrought havoc on the U-boat. We sailed through the Strait of Gibraltar at night and we were amazed to see the blazing lights of Tunis on our starboard side. To people who had left a blacked-out Britain and sailed through miles of ocean during nights of complete darkness it was truly a wonderful sight to see a city fully illuminated in a blaze of lights. I am sure that many in the convoy thought wistfully of the night when the lights would go on again at home.

Chapter 4

Ship-Building at Shandur

We sailed through the Mediterranean without any incident and docked at Alexandria 21 days after leaving Liverpool – there must have been 'slow coaches' in the convoy!

Many of the RAF personnel aboard transferred to a train bound for the south and as it was late evening we were disembarked at a tented camp somewhere south of Cairo. There was no platform; we just threw our kit onto the sand and jumped! The tent to which I was directed was a two man bell-tent and the only furnishing was an unlit storm lantern hanging from the tent pole. My tent- mate and I both dug a hollow in the soft sand, spread our ground-sheets in them, placed a haversack to act as a pillow and used our two blankets to act as bed clothes. Despite the heat of the day in Egypt and in other eastern countries it is surprising how cold it becomes during the night. When we had completed our domestic chores my mate said he was going for a walk and did I fancy going as well. I declined as I was going to write a letter home. I was not able to communicate with my home during our voyage. Off he went and that was the last I saw of him. Having written the letter I kipped down and was soon sound asleep. When I woke in the morning there was no sign of my tent-mate. I made enquiries and was told that he had been run over the previous night and that he had died. To my shame I do not even remember his name.

Next morning we continued our journey south and I and a few others were dropped at Shandur, an RAF station on the banks of the Great Bitter Lake. This camp was mainly occupied in training aircrew on Marauders, American planes with a tricycle undercarriage and not very popular with some aircrews. At Shandur work started early in the morning and finished about noon during the hot season and after lunch many airmen just flopped down on their beds and read or dozed off. Not so Jock Ward who came from Berwick, I think. First thing for him was to have a shave, shower and a shampoo, dress up in his best tropical kit and go for a walk round the camp. Perhaps later he would go to our cinema called 'Shaftos' with a packet of crisps and a bottle of Stella beer.

There was not much entertainment at Shandur and one day when a friend called Fazackerley and I happened to find a 16ft board, about 8 inches wide and half an inch thick, on the shore of the lake we decided to make a canoe. The rest of the canoe consisted of wooden engine crates and torn canvas engine covers which were u/s (unserviceable). Carpenter's tools were not found in abundance at an air-base but we managed to 'scrounge' sufficient for our requirements and when the skeleton was covered with canvas, the remaining essential component was 'dope' – a paint which shrank canvas and made our canoe as tight as a drum. We found this and after making a couple of double paddles with bamboo and plywood we were ready for sea! We had to forego any official launching as breaking the most fragile bottle over the bows of our canoe would have caused irreparable damage. Therefore we pushed off across the Great Bitter Lake without any formal ceremony!

We enjoyed many pleasant outings in our home made canoe often crossing to a small island at the edge of the Suez Canal where we could watch ships passing down towards Suez. The ships passing through the canal had to do so slowly otherwise the wash of the ship could seriously damage the canal.

Unfortunately, during one crossing, a strong wind suddenly blew up causing short but steep waves. Despite careful handling of the canoe, the bow happened to be on the crest of a wave while the stern was on the crest of another. Our combined weight in the middle caused the keel to snap but fortunately the 'doped' canvas held and we were able to nurse our flexible canoe back to terra firma. The canoe was not insured – so we declared it a write-off!

At Shandur our billets were Nissen huts built facing inwards in circles. Each was placed over a rectangular hollow made of bricks and with a concrete floor. This design must have been the work of an architectural crank or a genius – we were never sure which! The toilets and showers were about 100 yards away and as there were no females at all on the camp the airmen just stripped and walked naked to the showers carrying a towel over their shoulders and a precious soap held in their hands. I got quite a shock one day when I heard female squeals at first behind me and then alongside me as a truck full of ENSA artistes were on their way to the Officers' Mess. The driver had diverted from the straight (and narrow) route when he sighted me walking casually along in the buff! I never found out his identity!

The second boat-building venture in Shandur came about when I spotted the float of a seaplane lying behind a building. There was no sign of the rest of the seaplane and I did not ask any questions except one. I approached the Engineering Officer and asked him if I could convert the float into a dinghy. He looked at me with a puzzled and perhaps a sympathetic look thinking no doubt that the sun was beginning to affect my sanity. "Ok" he said, "but let me see the dinghy before you launch it." With help from other airmen who were probably trying to stake a claim for crew membership we managed to move the float to a more convenient spot out of sight of prying eyes!

During periods when I was off duty I began the conversion with very basic tools consisting of a hacksaw and a hammer and cold chisel. I will not go into

The Suez Canal and the Great Bitter Lake

details regarding procedures as they are copyright! Also I wished to be skipper of this craft! On the day of launching I forgot to tell the Engineering Officer as I thought he might be busy! In the meantime a few single paddles had been made and a few sandbags filled for ballast – there was plenty of sand available but the bags were not so plentiful!

We set off across the Lake with a following wind which was rising and when we were about halfway across I decided it would be advisable to head back to Shandur. Therefore I turned the craft to starboard as I had been taught in my youth in Lewis always to turn a boat 'deiseil' clockwise or sunwise: to ignore this custom could result in bad luck or worse! Now that we were facing the wind paddling became hard work and there were mutinous murmurings amongst the crew as they watched me apparently sitting idle at the tiller. I was no Captain Bligh but the leader of the 'mutiny' was a landlubber cocky Cockney – a "Fletcher Christian" who was demanding that the ballast be thrown overboard in order to lighten the craft. I advised strongly against doing this pointing out that if this were done we would capsize. Nonetheless, it was done and shortly afterwards we turned turtle. Fortunately we capsized over a sandbank and the Cockney who was a six-footer was able to stand with his head and shoulders above water but he was a non-swimmer! The rest of us managed to right the craft and empty it of most of the water and then we got the Cockney aboard after a struggle. We had also salvaged some of the paddles and we gave him one and told him to paddle for his life while we kept the craft from capsizing again by swimming alongside it. By the time we had covered the half mile or so to shore he was physically exhausted and a mental wreck as we were now in deep water – in more ways than one for him – and we, the crew had by now turned against him, threatened to abandon him unless he pulled harder on the paddle and taunted him about seamanship and the ability to swim!

After this fiasco I gave up shipbuilding!

One day a mate and I on our day off hitched a lift to Suez from Shandur and while walking along a street we noticed a shop that bore above the door 'JOCK MACGREGOR THE ONLY EGYPTIAN SCOTSMAN'. I said to my mate that we must go in and when we did I asked if I could see Jock. The attendant went in to the back of the shop and appeared with a very dusky Egyptian who spoke Broad Scots. Having bought a beautiful leather album from him I asked where he had learned the Scots tongue and he told me that some time before a Scots regiment had been stationed in Suez and he had learned it from them.

Shortly afterwards I was posted to Abu Sueir some distance to the North along with two others from Shandur, Paddy Neeson and an Aberdonian named Mackay. Our first encounter was with the Station Warrant Officer (SWO) who gave us a brief inspection and barked to Paddy, "Go and get a haircut and report to me when you've had one." When Paddy reported back, the SWO was flabbergasted because Paddy, who had a short fuse, had asked the barber to shave his head. The SWO then threatened to charge him with insubordination! You can't win with SWO's!

Now let me record an incident that occurred concerning another SWO at a station while I was stationed there. The SWO was of the same ilk as the rest of them and the internal telephone system was as temperamental as the SWO, hence the lines were tested frequently. During the lunchtime break the 'A' flight office was manned by only one airman whose duties were, inter alia, to usher an aircraft that happened to land to an appropriate hard standing. A certain LAC

This photo was taken by Archie Macphail in 1946 when we were on the package tour to Palestine. The location is at the North end of the Dead Sea near where the Bedouin shepherd, Muhammed edh-Dhib, discovered the Dead Sea scrolls in a cave at Qumran in 1947. Pity we did not go into the caves!

who was aware of the arrangement chose a favourable time to enter the office and he phoned the SWO announcing that he was the line-tester and would the SWO please repeat slowly after him: "What shall I do with my currant bun?" The SWO did so and the answer was abusive, unprintable but appropriate especially if one had been subjected to the dictatorial, ungrammatical ("Get fell in") and obnoxious orders of the said ignoramus! The 'line-tester' had taken precautions to avoid detection ensuring that he left no evidence behind – he spoke with a pebble in his mouth to garble his speech! Of course, the rank and file soon knew who the 'line-tester' was and no-one squealed and even now after over 60 years I shall not mention his name!

When it became my turn to be booked in at Abu Sueir I sat at a table along with a clerk who asked the usual questions among which was Name and Address. When I gave this the clerk booking someone in at the next table looked up and when I was about to leave he asked me, "Bheil Gàidhlig agad?" (Do you speak

Gaelic?) I replied in the affirmative and then he said, "I'll see you in the NAAFI at 7pm." This we did and Archie Macphail from Carinish, North Uist and I became firm friends. This was 1946 and as we were both due leave we decided to book a package tour to Palestine. This tour was very interesting and we were able to visit all the holy places including the Church of the Nativity, the Garden of Gethsemane and many more. One day we went down to the Dead Sea 1,100 feet below sea level and we went for a swim if one could call it that. The density of the water was so high that you could sit in it without sinking and it was so salty that if it got into your eyes you could not open them. When we were skimming around we heard frantic female cries not far away and when we arrived at the scene we found a young lady who had got water in her eyes and found she could not open them. She started screaming but we managed to get near her and told her we would keep on talking and guide her to the shore. When we got ashore a fresh-water tap was conveniently situated for such an emergency.

Not long after we came back off leave I was posted to Palestine; this was no package tour! The war in Europe had not long ended and hundreds of Jewish refugees were landing illegally in Palestine. At this time Britain had a mandate in that country and the Red Berets were sent there to maintain law and order. They faced opposition from the Irgun Zvai Leumi and the Stern Gang. There was also fighting especially in the north of Palestine and we were sometimes caught in the cross-fire between Jews and Arabs. On one occasion a friend and I were walking along a street and we heard a tremendous explosion, and then saw the front of St David's Hotel being blown into the street. Fortunately we were able to dodge back round the corner before the blast could hit us.

When I finished my tour in Palestine I was posted to Heliopolis near Cairo and I never saw Archie Macphail again. We had kept in touch by mail and in his last letter to me he was cock-a-hoop that he was on his way home for demobilisation but he did not make it – he took ill as the troopship approached the Clyde and died in a Glasgow hospital. I learned this sad news when I was a first year student at Glasgow University and residing in Macleay Hall. My informant was Archie MacVicar from North Uist who became a Church of Scotland minister and who was an excellent preacher.

In the 1990's Edward Young, retired Rector of The Nicolson Institute and I used to visit North Uist for a week's angling in May. Both of us were Associate Members of the North Uist Angling Club. and were very grateful to Philip Harding, Secretary of the Club. I told Philip about Archie and said I would be grateful if he could trace any relatives of Archie's still living. Philip was soon able to trace a sister and he took me to visit her. She was happy to see me and when I handed her a couple of photographs of Archie that I had taken in Palestine, she was both delighted and moved.

Chapter 5

A Recalcitrant Donkey

When I first arrived at Heliopolis I found it very different from Shandur which was an isolated base in the desert and from Palestine where there was constant tension because of the terrorist actions. In Heliopolis I learned that the previous Commander-in-chief of the RAF in the Middle East had been Lord Tedder and that his wife, Lady Tedder, had been killed in an air crash in North West Africa in a plane from this base. The subsequent Court of Enquiry found that the crash was due to engine trouble. Thereafter a ruling was made that the fitter servicing the Commander-in-Chief's plane had to fly in it but voluntarily. When I arrived at Heliopolis the Commander-in-Chief RAF Middle East was Sir Charles Medhurst and there was a vacancy for a fitter on his plane which was a Dakota. I volunteered and got the job.

One day the plane came in for servicing and when this was done an Air Test had to be carried out. When we were airborne I had to stand behind the pilots and check all gauges pertaining to the engines – oil pressure gauges, magnetos, etc. All was well and I sat in the back admiring the view as we came in to land over the Pyramids. There was a sudden thump and when we landed we found that a bird, probably a vulture, had collided with the port side of the nose just below the pilot's side window and caused considerable damage including the semi-destruction of the Commander-in-Chief's coat-of-arms. Panic stations! First of all the damaged section had to be removed which entailed removing hundreds of self-tapping screws and the same number had to be replaced when the replacement was carried out. There was no spare Dakota nose panel at Heliopolis and so urgent action had to be taken and one was located somewhere but when it arrived it still bore camouflage colours of brown and green. However, those were soon removed and it gleamed silvery bright just like the rest of the Commander-in-Chief's Dakota. All that remained to do was to re-paint the coat-of-arms using the damaged section as a guide. May I say here that I had nothing to do with the artwork! The end result was perfection itself and I doubt if Sir Charles was ever aware that his plane had a tussle with a bird!

The purpose of preparing the Dakota was to take Sir Charles to Ma'an in Jordon on his way to visit Petra. But it was discovered that the airstrip at Ma'an was rather short for a Dakota to use. Alternative plans were made and it was decided to use a smaller plane and so Lodestar AX723, with Flight-Lieutenant

McGillivray as pilot was chosen. He asked me to accompany him while he practised 'circuits and bumps' – that is to take off, make a circuit and then land. My function was to operate the undercarriage and flaps and when we came down, to run back to where we had landed and following the tyre marks – Helio had no runways, just the landing strip – and count the steps back to where the plane had stopped. We must have made a few circuits and bumps before the F/Lt was satisfied because my Log Book records Air Test 45 minutes! I must have been fit but again that was over sixty years ago! In the event he had no problems landing the Lodestar at Ma'an. From there we travelled in a truck and a Jeep across the desert to an Army outpost at Wadi Husa. On the way a halt was called and Sir Charles shared the rations provided for him among us all, and there was no segregation of ranks!

At Wadi Husa we were each given a donkey to transport us to Petra. The one allocated to me was the heftiest in the bunch but she had a follower upon which she doted and fed with commendable motherly care and love at very frequent intervals. We often fell behind the rest and this was neither safe nor advisable judging by the attitude of some natives in the settlements we passed through. I tried various means to coax my recalcitrant mount to keep up – such as kicking both heels in her flanks as I had seen some Arabs do, or cursing her in English which was quite ineffective. Then I tried cajoling her in Gaelic and off she went like a flash pushing all off the path until she came up behind Sir Charles and his donkey who were leading. That donkey must have been a high-ranking officer in the Donkey Fraternity because it would not give way and so my charge promptly tried to bite a chunk out of its rump! The victim made off with Sir Charles desperately trying to hang on and fortunately he did. At last the party halted and he turned round and said, "Who did that?" My donkey could not understand English, only Gaelic, and he was not enlightened!

When we arrived in Petra it was the most fantastic sight imaginable. According to information in Philips Atlas of the World it was the "Centre of the Nabataean kingdom from c 312BC to AD105". How people in those days and the limited tools available to them, could construct pillars of such size and beauty, together with the carvings on buildings, is mind-boggling. We made our way back from Petra to Ma'an without incident and then we took off for Heliopolis. In the meantime a young Pilot Officer, a relative of Sir Charles, took over the Second Pilot's seat. He was as different from Sir Charles as chalk is from cheese, but he soon got his comeuppance! It was dark when we came in to land at Heliopolis. He was able to select undercarriage down but as we were on the approach to land the pilot asked for quarter flaps he could not operate them. The result was that the landing had to be aborted and another circuit made. The Pilot signalled me to come and kneel beside the flaps lever where I could see the gauge which was numbered from zero to 360 with 25, 50 and 75 highlighted.

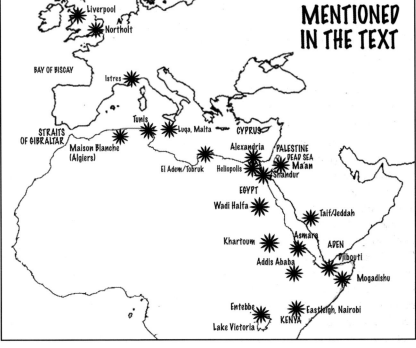

As we came in to land the Pilot shouted quarter flap, half flap, etc and I was able to select all without a problem. I knew Lodestar AX723 better than I knew my donkey! There was a slight technical snag in the flaps but the rigger who had not had time to rectify it before take-off, had showed me how to overcome it. I found him shortly after landing and as we both knew there would be an investigation, he took appropriate action as soon as possible. In the morning I got a message to report to the CO's office where W/C Woodward asked me to explain why I was able to operate the flaps and the second pilot could not. I replied that I did not know. He dismissed me with a cold look.

Shortly after arriving at Heliopolis I met Harold Smith from Standish near Wigan. He happened to occupy a bed next to me in the most luxurious billet I ever occupied in the RAF. It was a substantial two-storey concrete building and there was plenty of space to move around. Harold was better known as 'Ginger' because of his crop of red hair. His main interests were football and boxing, like myself, and we spent hours practising. One evening, boxing in the gymnasium I hurt him and he immediately retaliated, giving me a black eye and breaking my watch which I should not have been wearing! Unfortunately, I was due to fly out before dawn in Dakota KJ840 on 4/9/46 with the Station Commander W/C Duigan as Pilot – a very amiable Australian who had succeeded W/C Woodward. On getting back to our billet 'Ginger' who was a good watchmaker delved into his box of bits and pieces of watches and assembled a working model before lights out. I needed a watch as I had to record times of take-off and landing during our trip.

I got an early call in the morning and as soon as I had washed, shaved and dressed I woke Harold and got him to camouflage the damage he had caused the previous evening. He did such a good job with cream and talc that nobody noticed my black eye until the sun rose and the temperature along with it! Then my make-up ran down my face with the sweat! The Second Pilot remarked sarcastically: "We are going on a goodwill mission and you are going to arrive with a black eye!" However, things turned out differently.

We arrived at Taif via Jedda and first of all we were entertained in a large room where we were given countless small cups of tea which were delicious, but as soon as we emptied a cup it was immediately replenished. We discovered later that the only way to indicate that one had enough was to shake the cup and then it would be taken away. Later we were led into the dining room which was long and fairly narrow. The top table was occupied by Prince Mansua, the fourth son of King Ibn Saud and on each side of him were the dignitaries who attended the conference including W/C Duigan our CO. The rest of us were sitting along each side of the table with a Saudi Army officer on each side of us. One of the ones beside me spoke perfect English and he asked me how I came by my black eye. I told him a half-truth that I had been engaged in a boxing bout the previous evening in Cairo and when he asked me if I had won I assured him that I had! When I told this to Ginger he was furious!

During the course of the evening my Saudi neighbour at the table introduced me to some of his friends telling them about my victory the previous evening in Cairo. They showed great respect for me and while this was going on I noticed the Second Pilot watching proceedings. I caught his eye and winked at him with my black eye and he graciously winked back! So much for diplomatic missions! Behind each of the visiting party as we dined stood a guard carrying a vicious looking sword. We had been told beforehand that the more we ate the more pleased our hosts would be and the Wireless Operator who was sitting opposite me must have taken this to heart. At one stage he made a sudden movement with both hands to his waist to slacken his belt and the guard behind him immediately drew his sword thinking that perhaps he was going to draw a gun! The Wireless Operator was blissfully unaware of what had happened behind him and carried on enjoying his meal!

Chapter 6

Cricket Tour of East Africa and a Hebridean Hogmanay in County Durham

In the summer of 1946 there were still many Dakotas flying under the British flag and the Americans who produced them and used them in various campaigns were more or less finished with the European theatre of war. Therefore they were about to dump into the Mediterranean surplus military hardware including Dakota spares. The authorities at Heliopolis must have found this out and on 26/7/46 a Dakota KJ840 was dispatched to Maison Blanche, now a suburb of Algiers, with a skeleton aircrew and about half a dozen technicians who would choose which spares they considered necessary to salvage – a technical officer supervising operations.

Maison Blanche in July was a hot spot and we soon required a change of clothing. A group of us found a lady in the village nearby who took in laundry but she spoke only French! But never mind, the country bumpkin from the Western Isles came to the rescue! By pointing to the laundry and a little body language she understood what we required and she said enthusiastically, "Oui, Oui, Oui!" I tried out my pidgin French and the conversation went thus: Me: "Quand prêt?" She: "Vendredi". Me: "A quelle heure?" She: "A deux heures et demi." Me: "Très bon – bonjour, Madame." My mates who had stood open-mouthed listening to this international conversation must have felt that the yokel from the Outer Isles was a useful ancillary to have around!

By 30th July all the spares had been loaded on the Dakota and the pilot, suspecting that the plane was overloaded, decided to carry out an Air Test before heading for Heliopolis. He took me with him to operate the undercarriage and flaps and as Maison Blanche was situated with mountains all round it the pilot made a couple of circuits within the bowl and then came in to land as he could not gain sufficient height to clear the mountains. He ordered that a ton of spares be unloaded as there would be another extra seven airmen aboard when we took off for Heliopolis.

This was done and on the next day we left Maison Blanche for Heliopolis but on the way a technical hitch compelled us to divert to Luqa in Malta where we stayed overnight. A visit to the 'Gut' in Valetta was an eye-opener, a very run-down area, and not very safe although we did have strength of numbers having enlisted two brawny sailors to our party!

Next day we set off from Luqa to Heliopolis with the Form 700 duly signed

Cairo dinner to celebrate the Cricket Tour in East Africa – I am sixth from left

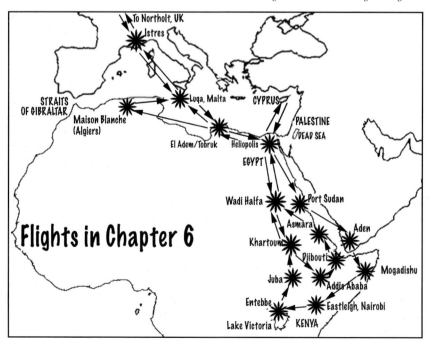

by a Luqa mechanic that the Dakota was airworthy. However, when we were more than half-way across the Med an oil-leak developed in the CSU (Constant Speed Unit) in the starboard engine – the oil showing on the engine nacelle. Having observed the amount of oil being lost which was not too serious, it was decided to head for El Adem in North Africa. There we topped up the oil-tank and made for Heliopolis where we landed after 10 hours flying from Maison Blanche via Malta.

Another adventurous trip I recall was a trip from Heliopolis to Nicosia, Cyprus with a load of convalescents who had succumbed after some years in the desert to ailments to which non-natives are often prone – blood disorders and tummy problems, etc. We were flying in Lodestar AX723, the plane that was often prone to hydraulic problems and there was no qualified aircrew aboard except the pilot who knew the route like the back of his hand and thus did not require a navigator nor a wireless operator. All the help he required was someone to operate the landing gear and the flaps on take-off and landing. Stevenson, a rigger, and I, a fitter, were aboard to perform those duties although one would normally have sufficed.

When we cleared the coast and were flying over the Med the pilot switched on "George" – the automatic pilot – and said he had to go to the toilet which was at the rear of the plane. He told me to sit in his seat; Stevenson was already in the co-pilot's seat and if we spotted any plane one of us had to go for him immediately. A few minutes after he had gone the plane started bucking up and down in an alarming way. I did not have a clue what caused this but Stevenson soon realised that there was an airlock in the hydraulic system and he switched off "George". Hydraulics were his department!

The pilot appeared and having closed the cabin door behind him stood for a moment flabbergasted and then hauled me out of his seat and grabbed the wheel and told Stevenson to let go. The pilot was so livid that he did not speak to us for a while – I think he was checking that we were still on course which we were and then he switched on "George" again. After a minute the Lodestar once again behaved like a Wild West steed at a Rodeo and the pilot had to switch off the recalcitrant auto-pilot.

I often wondered what the poor convalescents in the back thought of the whole performance. Did any of them perchance think it was a modern day type of therapy for upset stomachs or "Gyppo Guts" as the malady was called locally?

When we arrived at Nicosia the pilot had the decency to apologise and in fact congratulated us on taking the correct action under the circumstances. However, when the convalescents were disembarking Stevenson and I remained in the cockpit because first, we were returning immediately to Heliopolis and second, we did not wish to have to explain to them the therapy they received en voyage!

On 18th March 1946, Ventura JT817 took off from Heliopolis to Addis Ababa with the Archbishop of York. Fortunately the Pilot was Flying Officer Jepson who had spent some time in his youth in India where he was aware of cloud behaviour. As we flew south in a clear sky he spotted a solitary cloud ahead and surmised that there was a mountain there and he changed course from that prescribed although there was no obstacle marked at the height we were flying. It was just as well he changed course because as we passed by on one side of the cloud we caught a glimpse of a mountain top inside it higher than we were!

The Archbishop was accompanied by a Curate and they both wore clerical garb despite the heat. As the pilot had increased our flying altitude, the Archbishop required oxygen. With such an eventuality in mind the staff at Heliopolis had provided an oxygen cylinder and a mask and had given me two minutes tuition on how to operate it When the Archbishop asked for oxygen I appointed the Curate as my assistant! I gave him the mask and told him to fit it on to his boss and when this was done to signal me to turn on the gas. I did so on receipt of the signal but after a couple of minutes the Curate signalled for more and I turned the tap further on and waited! Sure enough after another couple of minutes came the signal for more and I made sure he got more! He whipped the mask off his face and handed it to the Curate who handed it to me not with anger, but I thought I detected a trace of a smile on his face!

The return route was changed probably so that we would avoid the necessity to fly at a high altitude to avoid any other uncharted mountains. From Addis Ababa we flew to Djibouti in French Somaliland where the temperature and humidity were very high. I asked the Curate if he and the Archbishop had tropical kit and he assured me that they had. When I asked him why they were not wearing it he replied that he would not wear it unless the Archbishop did. "Why not?" I asked. "Protocol" he said. From Djibouti we flew to Asmara in Eritrea where the airstrip was about 5000 feet above sea-level. It was somewhat disconcerting on take-off to see ground about 100 feet below and next moment about 5000 feet below! After a stop in Khartoum overnight we arrived in Heliopolis next day via Wadi Halfa.

On 15 October 1946 Dakota KJ840 with Pilot Flight-Lieutenant Howells took off from Heliopolis with a combined Services Cricket team from the Middle East which consisted of RAF and Army personnel, but there was no Royal Navy representative because their peripatetic life precluded them from being selected.

The leader of the team was Sir Brian Baker, depute CIC Middle East who was an enthusiastic and capable cricketer. Our itinerary was: Heliopolis>Port Sudan>Aden>Mogadishu>Eastleigh, Nairobi>Entebbe>Juba>Khartoum> Heliopolis. Cricket games were played at Aden and then we flew on to Mogadishu for refuelling. When a petrol bowser had finished refuelling I carried out the obligatory practice of opening the four draining cocks underneath the tanks to drain away any water condensation since the previous refuelling. Many mechanics overlooked the instruction as usually the amount of water forming in the tanks was negligible, but fortunately I did not. The fuel cocks were locked with copper wire which had to be cut starting at No.1 and the tap opened. This procedure was followed with the other three drain-cocks. The way to differentiate water from petrol was to let what emerged from the tap flow into the palm of your hand and if it was water it would bubble and if it was petrol it would not.

After the refuelling bowser had filled the four tanks which could hold 802 gallons all told, I started the checking procedure and found that it was water that was flowing from the tanks. I turned all the taps off and went to find the Station Engineering Officer. When he came along and saw the amount of liquid on the concrete hard-standing he frowned and told me to turn on the taps again. He tested each tank and immediately agreed that it was water and not petrol that was emerging. He told me to close all taps and soon an empty bowser came and sucked the tanks dry. Another bowser, hopefully with unadulterated petrol, was standing by and filled up.

Before take-off I asked the Engineering Officer to confirm that all we had in our tanks was petrol. Fortunately I had gone by the book and when we did check we found that it was petrol that emerged from the tanks. As petrol is lighter than water it rises to the top and so should we have taken off without carrying out the check we would probably have flown for some time but not for the three and three quarter hours it took us to fly to Eastleigh – there would have been another mystery air-crash in the jungles of Africa. The message is: "Always go by the book!"

Some time after getting back to Heliopolis I asked the pilot if he knew how the water could have got into the first consignment of fuel we had received at Mogadishu. He told me that the petrol for Mogadishu came from a port, Beira further south in Mozambique and that it was transported north in 50 gallon drums in trucks driven by Italian POWs. He also told me that some of the drivers used to sell some of it on the way north and top up the drums with water! He thanked me for probably saving all our lives but told me to keep it under my hat as enquiries were still ongoing. I was grateful for his appreciation and thanks as that was the only gratitude ever expressed to me over the matter. Having arrived safely in Kenya, which at that time had a strong English presence, the pilot asked the crew diplomatically to attend as many matches as possible to support our team as probably we would be the only support they would have. But not so; the spectators were very sporting and applauded good play on both sides.

During our stay from the 17th to 24th October a group of us, both players and crew, decided to go on safari at dawn to the Athi Plain. Fortunately the truck we were in was driven by a native who knew what to do when an emergency arose. On arrival at a native settlement we tried to make friendly contact with the residents but the females seemed to treat us as strange apparitions and stood peering at us round the corners of their huts giggling all the time and if we looked their way they would scream and run out of sight. An Army Officer, a member of the team, began conversing in sign language with a tall handsome male who was the Chief, according to the driver. The Officer took out a packet of cigarettes from his pocket, stuck one in his own mouth and offered the Chief one. He took it and placed it in his own mouth and then began chewing it! The Officer lit his own cigarette with a lighter but he had to give the Chief another cigarette as the first one was unsmokeable!

Shortly after moving away from the settlement we came across a number of giraffes and the driver stopped the truck. Giraffes by nature seem to be very curious and they moved slowly towards the truck but when they were quite close they decided they had seen enough and ran away with their long necks swaying up and down gracefully. Soon we came across a rhinoceros which was about 50 yards away. On spotting us, he raised his head and took aim! Then he lowered his head and charged. The driver had placed the truck at right angles to its path and when it was about 25 yards away the RAF pilot raised his camera and said "I'm taking a photo of this even if it's the last thing I do!" When it was about 15 yards away or maybe less the driver just moved the truck out of the way and that lethal hunk of flesh and bone went hurtling past at about 30 mph and crashed into a clump of trees probably stunning itself – we did not wait to check! It was then back to cricket.

After leaving Kenya our next 'port of call' was Entebbe in Uganda. The landing facilities there in those days were pretty basic – just a mown area of grass which acted as an air-strip. As there was no RAF presence there the crew and team were billeted in pairs with local residents. The Navigator and I were fortunate to find ourselves staying with Mr Drechfield who was a barrister and a bachelor and the owner of a yacht!

On one occasion he took the two of us out on Lake Victoria and he asked the Navigator to take with him his sextant so that we could swim on the Equator. The Navigator soon found the Equator and Mr Drechfield hove to and we took turns to go swimming always leaving one person aboard as a precaution in case the helm should jam.

Having enjoyed a very pleasant swim in the warm waters, we set off to the northern end of the Lake which was dotted with small islands on which crocodiles lay with their mouths wide open while white birds stood beside them, busily picking their teeth and enjoying a luscious meal from the crocodiles' last victims! The Navigator and I looked at each other and shuddered! We asked

Mr Drechfield if it had been safe to go swimming when there were crocodiles about; he assured us it had been perfectly safe as crocodiles always stayed near the shore and we had been far from the shore. Amen!

Each morning I had to go to the plane to start the engines and run them up at high revs to keep the batteries charged. The first morning when I arrived at the Dakota there was a guard there with a rifle and bayonet. He looked somewhat menacing but he spoke no English and I showed him the keys of the plane. As I was afraid that if I left him outside he would have been killed by one of the propellers when I switched on, so I opened the door and beckoned him to go inside and I made him sit beside me on the floor in the cockpit. From his position he could only see the sky and when I opened the throttles to test the instruments the Dakota shuddered and vibrated. I had to prolong the exercise to allow the generators to charge the batteries. When I switched off we both left the plane but he had been convinced that we had been airborne and began clapping me on the back showing his appreciation!

On the second occasion I went to start the engines I was wearing shorts and I decided to take a short-cut across grass which was knee-high. Half-way across I remembered a story Mr Drechfield told us the evening before, and I started running. He had explained how he was going for a bath and his terrier was with him. As soon as he opened the bathroom door the terrier stood still and his hair stood on end. Mr Drechfield knew that something was wrong and he went back to fetch his revolver. When he opened the bathroom door again he saw a deadly snake crawling out from underneath the bath. He shot it dead. As the house was completely sealed with strong steel mesh and the only door was also covered in steel mesh and was spring-loaded so that it would close immediately behind one, he assumed that the snake had been planted when he was at work.

"Who would do that" we asked. "Well" he said, "I had sacked a house-boy a few weeks before and I suspect that he was responsible but I have no proof."

When I told Mr Drechfield that I had started running on the way to the plane he told me that was the last thing I should have done; I should have walked slowly stamping my feet and should a snake be in the vicinity it would slither away. Normally a snake only attacks when taken by surprise – point taken and lesson learned!

On 29th December 1946 Dakota KJ981 flew from Heliopolis to Northolt with a delegation representing the Royal Navy, the Army and the Royal Air Force to attend a conference in London – the Pilot was Sq/Leader Hartley.

The RAF delegate was Air Vice Marshal Sir Brian Baker, whom I knew from the cricket tour. The other two delegates were an Army Brigadier and a Naval Rear Admiral. Although the Dakota had about ten double seats the delegates chose to sit apart, each occupying a double seat by himself.

As the Dakota had no cooking facilities I was issued, before leaving Heliopolis, with two large insulated urns, one marked TEA and the other marked COFFEE. Also included were a couple of boxes, one with sandwiches and the other with biscuits. On a signal from the cockpit I was supposed to serve this 'repast' to the dignitaries aboard. When the signal came and as I had not received any instructions regarding protocol, I served the Air Vice Marshal first and since the Naval potentate had given me an ugly glare, I served him last!

The first two chose tea which I duly served to them but the Navy chose coffee. I went to the urn distinctly marked COFFEE, filled a cup and handed it to the Rear Admiral.

"That's not coffee" he barked at me "that's tea!"

"If it is, Sir, it came out of the urn marked COFFEE and I did not fill the urns!"

Another baleful glance at me and the order "Take it away!"

After my culinary duties had been completed the Air Vice Marshal who was sitting a few seats in front of me on the port side of the plane turned round and beckoned me to come up and sit beside him. The Naval Officer sitting almost opposite me across the aisle started to get out of his seat but the Air Vice Marshal with a gesticulation soon made it clear to whom he was signalling.

I went and sat beside him and noticed that he was reading "In Search of Scotland" by H. V. Morton. He told me that he intended to retire soon and that he wished to do some fishing in Lewis. Could I recommend some good fishing? I could and I did but I told him that it would be advisable to book early. He asked me which flies I would recommend for (a) sea trout and (b) salmon in Lewis and I was able to tell him.

When I met Sq Leader Murdo Macleod – he had been promoted from F/LT which was his rank when I met him in Arbroath – I told him the story. He told me that just before Air Vice Marshal Baker had retired he met him at Turnhouse, Edinburgh and some time later a basket of sea-trout arrived by air at the Officer's Mess at Turnhouse. Murdo and I surmised that they had come from Sir Brian and very likely they did.

As a matter of interest the route and the times taken were as follows:

29/12/46	Heliopolis- El Adem	03.00
	El Adem-Luqa	04.20
30/12/46	Luga-Istres	04.40
	Istres-Northolt	04.20

(Heliopolis is in Egypt. El Adem is in N Africa. Luqa is in Malta. Istres is in France).

The total number of flying hours from Heliopolis to Northolt was 16hrs

20mins in a Dakota and over two days. Present-day commercial flights do it in six hours!

When we landed at Northolt the crew were called together and told that as it was expected we would be flying back in four days we must not go beyond a 48-hour rail journey from London and we were given a telephone number to which we had to report every morning at 9am.

When I realised that I could not possibly get home and this was over two years since I had boarded the 'Alcantara' in Liverpool, I had a feeling of frustration tinged with sadness and perhaps a little homesickness, which I had sworn I would resist from the very day I joined the RAF. Once while at Shandur I was working on a plane and an Irishman older than I was came up to me and said "Jock, can you tell me where Ireland is?" I looked at my watch and then I looked at the sun and told Paddy to stand beside me and I pointed out with the utmost confidence where Ireland lay. Paddy, who had been watching the Arabs kneeling at certain times of the day paying obeisance to their deity did likewise to Ireland. When he rose there was a look of gratitude and serenity on his face and he thanked me profusely.

At Northolt, having cleared my head from all pessimism and creeping homesickness, I suddenly remembered the kind invitation that Mrs Bagnall had given me in 1944 when my pal Gordon Shepherd and I met by chance herself and her daughter Joyce who was Gordon's girlfriend. I wrote her address on a scrap of paper and handed it to the Orderly Clerk asking him to make out a return travel warrant for me, which he did. It was fairly late in the evening but I made it as far as Leeds that night.

Early next morning I set off by train to the north and eventually boarded a bus at Crook, County Durham which was to pass Roddymoor road end. The conductress kindly agreed to inform me when we reached the road end. By now it was pitch dark and when I stepped out of the brightly lit bus there were lights to the right of me, lights to the left of me and lights in front of me, but unlike Tennyson's description of the Charge of the Light Brigade they did not volley or thunder as the Russian cannon had. After the bus pulled away I noticed a blurred figure standing at the roadside and I approached and said "Excuse me." Next moment I was clutched and embraced and addressed "It's you after all, Mac!" What a happy coincidence!

We set off blithely for Roddymoor and about half a mile away we came to 7 Chestnut Grove where the Bagnalls lived; it was a few hours before the end of 1946. After I had partaken of very welcome sustenance, Mr & Mrs Bagnall, their family Joyce and Harry and I conversed happily until midnight when they told me that for the last thirteen years a family friend had been first-footing them. However, since he had not turned up by midnight I was given a piece of coal, sent out by the back door, told to go round to the front door and knock hard on it and first-foot them. The fact that at that time I was very fairhaired thanks to my genes and to the hot Middle East sun did not seem to deter them.

When I was admitted I handed over the piece of coal but then was at a loss as to what to do next. Suddenly I remembered our custom as youngsters in Balallan, Isle of Lewis when we used to go round the village reciting a Hogmanay ditty in Gaelic outside the doors. Hogmanay was the 12th of January and regarded in olden times as New Year. The leader of the group had a sheepskin tied to his back (usually with a pillow under it!) and on entry to the thatched house which in the old days had the fire in the middle of the floor, he had to go round the fire clockwise or sunwise three times while the man of the house hit him on the back with the long tongs which were always an adjunct to the hearth in those days. I recited the Hogmanay rant in Gaelic – as shown on the opposite page – in 7 Chestnut Grove, Roddymoor as the year 1947 was born. I wonder if it was ever recited before or after in County Durham!

As instructed I was to telephone a number in London every morning at 9 am to check on take-off time but just as happened recently in 2006/07 that city was fogbound and flying was out of the question. Although we were supposed to fly out on the 3rd of January, it was on the 9th January that we were eventually able to take off. The return flight was without incident as I made sure I had an urn of tea and an urn of COFFEE!

Before leaving, I gave Mrs Bagnall, who was a devoted member of the Baptist Church, my mother's name and address in Lewis and they started a correspondence which lasted until my mother died in 1984. Thereafter my wife Margaret and I continued the correspondence and during a bus-tour to Scarborough in the 1980's we travelled on a free day to meet Mrs Bagnall who was living in a sheltered home near Bishop Auckland, where I met her for the last time.

'S lèir dhomh tulach

'S lèir dhomh tràigh

'S lèir dhomh na fir air an t-sràid;

Taobh an fhearcain, taobh a phlocain,

Nochd oidhche na deagh bhinn air an uinneig;

Thàinig mi gu modhail eòlach an am tòiseachdain na Callainn

Cha leig thu leas sin innse dhomh, bha i ann bho linn mo sheanair;

Craicionn caorach 'na mo phòcaid, 's math an treòir a thig bhon fhear ud.

Leis an Achd a th'anns an dùthaich chan'eil dùil againn ri drama;

Ach rud beag de mhath an t-Samhraidh ma tha e ann cuir a mach e;

Bhean an taigh theirig suas, geàrr cùl càbaig is na geàrr aghaidh d'òrdaig;

Thoir an leòr do mhuinntir an taigh is thoir a bhonnag dhomhsa;

Gabhaidh sinn an t-aran gun an ìm, is gabhaidh sinn an t-ìm gun an aran;

Gabhaidh sinn a chàis leatha fhèin carson a rèist a bhiodh sinn falamh:

Ach aon rud a tha mi ag àicheadh dhut – siolagan de bhuntàta carrach;

Chan eil iad furasd' an giùlan, chan eil iad sunndach 's chan eil iad fallain,

Is cumaidh iad seachd tràth gun èirigh am Fear is treuna 'th'anns a bhaile.

THA A' CHALLAINN AN SEO.

If we received something the house was blessed thus:-

"Beannaichte gun robh an taigh is na th' ann eadar chrodh is eich is chaoraich is slàinte dhaoine gu robh ann"

On the very rare occasion that we were chased away the following malediction was pronounced:-

"Gum biodh do mhionach aig na starragan air na feannagan ro Latha Fheill Brìde!"

DUAN NA CALLAINN

The first five lines don't make much sense to me but the rest roughly translated is as follows:

I have come well-behaved and acquainted at the beginning of Hogmanay.

You need not tell me that it existed from my grandfather's day.

A sheepskin in my pocket, great is the strength that emanates from that one!

Because of the Act that prevails we do not expect a dram!

But a little of the produce of Summer if you have it dish it out

Housewife go up, cut the back of a cheese kebbock but not your thumb:

Give their fill to the household and give to me the bannock.

We'll take bread without butter, and we'll take butter without bread

We'll take cheese by itself and so why should we go empty-handed.

But one thing I forbid is small scraggy potatoes as they are not easy to carry, they give no vigour nor are they healthy and they will keep a-bed for a week the sturdiest fellow in the village.

HOGMANAY IS HERE

Blessing if we received something-

Blessed be this house and all it contains including cows, horses and sheep and may the people who dwell in it enjoy good health.

Malediction if we were turned away empty-handed – a very rare occurrence-

May the crows have your intestines on the lazy-beds before St Bride's day

Chapter 7

A Worrying Telegram

After a few months of complete boredom while awaiting the provision of transport to get home for demobilisation tension grew because of the apparent lack of interest on the part of the authorities to see us back home.

At last transport was arranged to convey us back to Liverpool in March 1947, this time on the 'Devonshire', a troopship about half the size of the 'Alcantara' on which I had gone out, also from Liverpool. Instead of making directly for Gibraltar, the Captain of the 'Devonshire' came near land halfway up the coast of Spain and sailed slowly southwards. No explanation was given and as some on board admired the beautiful Costa Blanca and the Costa Del Sol, others were becoming impatient and they used to assemble on deck and give a raucous rendering of 'The Slow Boat to China'. This made the Captain speed up but when we entered the Bay of Biscay no-one was singing. He had been biding his time providing us with a panoramic view of eastern Spain while a ferocious gale was raging in the Bay. When we did enter the Bay the Captain, unless he was a saint, must have been smiling sardonically as he surveyed the prostrate, seasick, semi-conscious 'corpses' strewn about the ship probably wishing they *were* on the Slow Boat to China!

Shortly after I arrived in Liverpool I stopped playing the part of "the soldier full of strange oaths etc." as I was demobilised on the 23rd of March 1947. The next step on the stage of life, according to Shakespeare was "the Justice in fair round belly with eyes severe etc." In my case, in lieu of Justice substitute Teacher because I didn't become a Justice until much later on. As regards the round belly, it took some time to develop, but his 'eyes severe' are part and parcel of the Teacher's armament – ask former pupils!

As it was apparent that I could not continue with my education until October of that year when Glasgow University would be taking in a new entry of students, I decided that I would try to supplement the meagre gratuity of £49 which was my reward for four years service in the RAF. I wrote to the Board of Trade and informed them that I wished to spend my gratuity by purchasing Harris Tweed yarn to enable me to earn some money as I was presently unemployed. I got a reply authorising me to purchase yarn from any of the Stornoway Tweed mills.

I approached one of them and asked to buy £50 worth of Harris Tweed yarn. The salesman at the desk looked at me with a supercilious smile on his face and said: "Oh, you can't get that!" "Oh, can't I?" was the reply as I produced the Board of Trade letter from my pocket and changed my tone to that of an SWO's! He read the letter and asked me to wait as he went to consult higher authority. He came back and said that on this occasion my request would be granted but that they would have to look into the matter.

"Right" I said, "let me see your yarn patterns" again the SWO's voice which I could imitate to perfection! I chose a beautiful blue Lovat and when the time came to sell the tweed I got top export price for it which I think was 17/6 per yard of three feet. I have heard of a baker's dozen which is 13, but why should a weaver's yard be 8 feet instead of 3 feet when the tweed is being woven and the weaver is paid per 8 foot yard?

My father had a loom and a handmade warping frame and so I was able to warp the tweed and weave it myself. Apart from the £50 worth of yarn I bought the profit from the sale was entirely mine except for a token charge I paid for washing and finishing it.

In October 1947 when I became a student at Glasgow University I found it very difficult to settle down after four-and-a-half year's absence from my studies, often in situations not conducive to academic pursuits. However, I did graduate M.A. and having finished my Teacher Training Course in Jordanhill, I applied for a post in Lewis and I was offered an interim job at Knock School, Point, which I gladly accepted. By this time I was romantically involved with a girl from Balallan, Margaret Maciver. When I got the letter from Dr George Thompson, the then Director of Education for Ross and Cromarty confirming my appointment, I immediately made for Charing Cross Post Office and sent Margaret a two-word telegram: "DOMUM IAIN" which in Latin meant "Going Home, Iain" – telegrams were charged by the word and money was scarce! The Post Office, probably due to ignorance of Latin or possibly not being used to such terse communications, changed it into a three-word telegram which gave it a completely different and more sinister meaning: "DO MUM, IAIN"!

In those days when telephones were few and far between, a telegram, apart from times of weddings, was often the harbinger of bad news. As Margaret was teaching at the time, her mother opened the telegram and got the shock of her life! When Margaret came home from school, despite the fact that she had passed Higher Latin in The Nicolson Institute, it took her some time to convince her mother that the telegram contained good news and not a threat to her welfare from her prospective son-in-law!

In my euphoria at being successful in obtaining a teaching post in Lewis I saw the poetic muse waving at me, albeit from a distance, and I composed and sent Margaret the following ditty:

TIGHINN A THEAGAISG A LEODHAS/
COMING TO TEACH IN LEWIS

Tha mòran, mòran sòlais an teachdaireachd mo dhàn ,

Tha m'inntinn tais mar chrònan is tha mo chridhe làn

De ghaol 's de ghean tha gasda, de chaidreamh agus tlàths,

Don ribhinn shnasail ghasda, 's e cridhe a cridhe blàths.

Rough Translation

There is abundant happiness in the message of my song

My mind is purring softly and my heart is full of love

Of fondness, friendship and tender pleasantness

For the elegant maiden, the heart of her heart is warmth.

Air maduinn toiseach Earraich 's mi 'm baile mòr na smùid,

Gun d'fhuair mi litir cheanalta bho MhacThòmais, Ph.D.

Ma bha mi gun chas-mhaid' orm gun leth-shùil no T.B.

*Gum faodainn dhol a theagaisg a dh'eilean suairc mo chrìdh.

On a morning in early Spring when I was in the foggy city of Glasgow

I received a kind letter from George Thomson Ph.D.

If my limbs were sound, I was not one-eyed or suffering from TB

I could go and teach in 'Eilean suairc mo chridhe' (Lewis)

Gu grad chaidh mi air ghluasad gu fios chur gu mo ghràdh.

Is abair cathair-shiabain 's mi gabhail sios an t-sràid.

A'lorg am facal Ladainn a dh'innseadh don te bhàn

Mar dhèilig ruinn am Freasdal 's mi nis dol thuic thar sàil.

Immediately I moved to send the good news to my love,

And what a mad rush as down the street I sped,

Searching for a Latin word that might be in my head,

To inform Margaret how Fate with us had dealt, I was now on my way across the seas to be beside her.

Cha bhliadhna nis gach seachdain oir tha mi faisg air làimh,

'S nuair tha mo chridhe aognaidh gun tèid mi na mo dheann

Gu ainnir a chùil dualaich, gu Màiread riòmhach chiùin,

'S gu faigh mi furan fàilteach bhom ghràdh don tug mi ùidh.

Each week is not like a year now that in Lewis I reside,

And when my heart is yearning I rush at full speed,

To the curly headed maiden, the lovely placid Màiread,

And I aye receive a welcome greeting from my love whom I adore.

*Before being granted a teaching post I had to provide a Medical Certificate confirming that I did not suffer from any physical handicap.

My appointment to Knock was a temporary one – the last term of session 1951-52 – but I shall never forget the beautiful scenery as I travelled by bus from Stornoway of a morning down the Braighe, nor will I forget the kindness and hospitality accorded to me by the parents in Point during my short stay there. On one occasion I was invited to Alexander 'Muirneag' Macleods' house for a meal while I was waiting to take the Knock School football team to play some other local team. During my visit, the 'old boy' took me to his private room where he spread the plans of the famous old fishing boat (from which he got his nickname) on the floor and regaled me with stories of good days and bad days in pursuit of the 'silver darlings'. I still meet his grandson Calum occasionally and will always remember his mental acuity in solving mathematical teasers. He gave the right answer to this one within two minutes. "John is twice as old as Mary was when John was as old as Mary is. John is 21. How old is Mary?" Try it in your spare time!

After leaving Knock I taught for four years in Laxdale School travelling daily with that expert and intrepid driver Ruairidh Uilleam 19 Balallan. He was always a skilful driver but he excelled himself driving in winter road conditions that the present generation cannot visualise. I was very sad when Roddy passed away at the early age of 57 years.

In 1956 I moved to Leurbost School. My happiest days in teaching were there both as an assistant teacher with John Murdo Macmillan as Head and also when I took over as Head Teacher in 1971. John Murdo had a very keen sense of humour which as a rule was applied to any pupils who broke the school regulations in any way – for example, one pupil whom he caught smoking was immediately baptised 'Woodbine' which nomenclature remained with him as long as he remained with us and perhaps for the rest of his life! It did not pay to break the rules in Leurbost School!

When I became the Head Teacher, the Junior Secondary curriculum was being replaced by the new system of Comprehensive Education. This new system meant that we had to adhere to a revised curriculum which was more restrictive than that which prevailed under the Junior Secondary regime when the less academic pupils were given special training in trades such as weaving and seamanship for the boys and pre-nursing or secretarial courses for the girls. To my mind the Junior Secondary system had advantages in that pupils could fulfil their potential in this way.

During my my early years there, John Murdo Macmillan and I decided that we would undertake a project connected with Crofting through which academic subjects would also be taught. The opportunity arose when at that time the Leurbost Grazings Committee had applied for 50 acres of the Common grazings to re-seed it and thus improve it for communal use. They were required to measure and mark out the appropriate acreage and submit a sketch to the

Crofters Commission. This they did and officials came to examine their handiwork but unfortunately the officials firmly asserted that the crofters had marked out an area which far exceeded the stipulated 50 acres. Thereupon the Grazings Committee approached the School, posed their problem to us and asked if we could help out. We could and we did.

Our first priority was to acquire the necessary equipment to perform the work accurately. We got a chain – 22 yards – and this would be far more accurate than a tape as it would follow the contours in the terrain. We also got proper marking posts and Neil Macleod, Keose, our teacher of technical subjects, constructed an ingenious theodolite which incorporated a capillary tube about 10 inches long from the Science lab, a protractor, a spirit-level and an ingenious system which provided vertical and horizontal movement which could be recorded in degrees. A lab stool served as a tripod for the theodolite. By pushing the legs of the stool into the peat and by use of the spirit-level the theodolite could be placed in a perfectly horizontal plane. Thus equipped John Murdo and his squad were able to produce a plan of the area in dispute and confidently announced that it was definitely less than 50 acres. The officials were informed and they thoroughly scrutinised the diagrams but could find no flaw in the calculations and so they had to concede defeat. What else could they do? It would have cost a bomb to disprove the School's findings! Leurbost Grazings Committee were very grateful and the School's reputation was much enhanced!

I also recall another innovation that took place in Leurbost School during the Junior Secondary era. With memories of my own school days in The Nicolson Institute when we were operating under a strict regime which did not encourage self-expression, I decided to form a School Club based on constitutional principles and consisting of an Executive Committee with a Chairman elected by the pupils from Class S3, the senior class in the School.

I remember a very competent Chairman we had – Donald John Macleod (Dòmhnull Iain Thormoid Càrnaidh) from Leurbost. He became a psychologist and is still sometimes heard on Gaelic radio. Members of the Club were also responsible in rotation for the School tuck-shop where biscuits and soft drinks were sold. When a consignment was sold out I could check from the proceeds that things were in order and they invariably were. If business petered out before the end of a meeting I would invite someone to come to the table and sing a Gaelic song. Our present Postmistress in Balallan, Cathie A Macaulay, would often volunteer and I feel that apart from the entertainment she provided it engendered complete self-assurance, a trait which she still possesses!

That concludes the fifth age of Shakespeare's actors on the Stage of Life. "The sixth shifts into the lean and slippered pantaloon (old fool) with spectacles on nose and pouch on side, his youthful hose well saved a world too wide for his shrunk shank etc." What a sad picture!

Chapter 8

The Theory of Probability and Guardian Angels

Once I retired I took Gaelic classes for a year in Gravir and in Comhairle nan Eilean in order to soften the transformation from academic pursuits to physical ones. At the end of that transformative year I felt fit and able to engage in my favourite sport of angling with the same enthusiasm and dedication which I hope I had applied to my academic career.

I bought a two-berth cabin cruiser which I named 'Girl Pat' after our youngest daughter Patricia. It was berthed in the sheltered bay in Keose and from there a friend and I would venture forth to fertile fishing grounds in the vicinity of Calbost Bay and Kebbock Head.

I remember Norman Mackenzie, my good friend from Keose and I filling three baskets with prime fish of nine different varieties including a conger eel of 24 lbs caught by Norman. When it managed to wriggle off the gaff and shared our smallish well-deck with us we had some exciting moments before we were able to render it harmless!

All our fish were rod caught in depths ranging from 20 to 30 fathoms. It was after one of those fishing expeditions that I composed the poem Calbost, included on Page 58 and dedicated to Calum Morrison, hero of the 'Arlington Court'. Calum Morrison was only 17 years old when the Germans torpedoed his ship the 'Arlington Court' in mid Atlantic. The survivors took to the lifeboats but there was no-one aboard the lifeboat in which Calum was who could handle a sailing boat except himself. He took charge of the boat and the sharing of the food and water aboard. He had been at the helm of the 'Arlington Court' shortly before she was sunk and decided to follow the course she was then steering as he correctly surmised that she was heading for a shipping lane. He spent five days and five nights at the helm and then they were rescued by a Norwegian ship. He got a medal for his bravery and seamanship.

In my younger days there was a rowing boat in practically every second croft in Balallan and the same applied to all the other villages in Kinloch. They were used mainly for hand-line fishing – dorghach – and one did not have to spend long at a recognised fishing spot – oitir – to fill a basket of prime fish including haddock, codling, flounders, whiting etc. These recognised fishing spots have been marked on a map of the loch by the Kinloch Historical Society and among

Calbost

A-mach mu Eilean Chalabraigh
Bha ceilearadh air eòin;
Bha'n iarmailt 's i cho annasach
'San loch gu lèir cho ciùin;
Bha rionnach air an adhar
Agus currag air tìr mòr,
Bha sgòthan bàn a' seòladh àrd
Thar baile breagha Chromòir.

'Cur cùl ri Eilean Thabhaigh
Bha'n cuan le began buinn,
Briseadh cùl na Dubh-sgeire
Ceann-uidh' nan iomadh tonn;
Mu choinneamh Mol nam Bràithrean
Bha 'ghaoth air teannadh cruaidh,
Bha Chàbag chas air fàir gu deas
'S i coinneachadh nan stuadh.

'S iomadh sàr a dh'àraicheadh
Mu chladaichean ri'r taobh,
A bha air sàl roimh iomadh nàmh
A' seòladh feadh an t-saoghail;
Bha cuid a sheall an treubhantas,
Mar Chalum òg air stiùir,
Nuair shàbhail e a chompanaich
Le ealantas is iùil.

'S ann an Calabost a rugadh e
'Sa fhuair e teagaisg òg,
Seòladh mach o Gheodha 'n Duilisg
Is Eilean beag a' Ghò;
Dh'fhàg sin a làmh cho ealanta
Nuair bha iad ann an càs,
Nuair dhìobair balaich Shasainn bhochd
Nach togadh seòl air bàt'.

Thug e iad gu sàbhailte troimh' n
A' ghaillinn is droch là,
Gus' n ràinig iad an caladh sin
Far 'n do fhreasgair orra bàt;
Ma thèid thu 'n diugh a Chalabost
Chan fhaic thu idir suinn,
Chan eil fòr air luchd na mara ann,
'Na seòid a' sheòl na tuinn.

Here is a rough translation:

Out by Calabrigh Isle the birds were in full song;
The sky looked unusual and the loch was like a pond;
Above us was a mackerel sky and the mainland was capped with mist,
White clouds were sailing high o'er the bonny village of Cromore.

As we left Tavay Isle there was quite a ground swell,
Which broke against the Dubh-Sgeire the destination of many a billow;
Opposite the Brothers' Shingly Beach the wind had grown strong,
Steep Kebbock Head was far to the south meeting the high billows.

Many a hero was born and raised on the shores nearby,
Who was at sea facing many a foe as they sailed the Seven Seas;
Some showed their valour, like young Calum at the helm,
When he saved his mates with skill and grit.

It was in Calbost he was born and learned his skill,
Sailing out from Geodha 'n Duilisg and Eilean beag a' Ghò;
That's what left his hand so skilful when they were in dire distress,
When the poor English lads could not hoist a sail to mast.

He took them safely through storms and bad days,
Until they reached their destination where a ship came to their aid;
If today you go to Calbost you will not meet with any heroes,
There is no sign of those stalwarts, the braves who sailed the waves.

them is one known as Aite na Caillich – The Place of the Old Lady. On the Laxay shore opposite this 'oitir' is a hill known as Airde na Caillich and the story associated with it as follows.

One evening at dusk an old lady from Laxay was 'buachailleachd a' chruidh' – herding the cattle – and in her dark clothes she was perfectly camouflaged when a rogue from the south side of Loch Erisort came ashore and captured a calf which belonged to the old lady and put it into his boat. Naturally the old lady intervened but she was murdered and dumped overboard halfway across the loch. Much later on, three men were hand-line fishing and the boat owner brought aboard a bone which he promptly threw back into the sea. Minutes later, he brought the bone aboard again and passed it on to one of his mates, told him to hold it and then pass it on to the third man. When this man took hold of the bone it spurted blood. He was the murderer and hence the two place names!

Norman Mackenzie from Keose and I were fishing at Aite na Caillich one cold Saturday evening. We always found that the best time to go fishing in Loch Erisort was at the end of the ebb tide, and when the tide began to flow the fish always seemed to follow the tide

While it was still ebbing, there was little activity and in order to keep the circulation going we opened a gill of Trawler Rum. The blue plastic label round the top of the bottle bore the name 'Watson of Aberdeen' and it was torn off in two pieces which were thrown overboard in about 10 to 12 fathoms of water.

We had a good catch for a couple of hours after the tide had turned and all the fish were thrown into a basket which we had in the boat. The catch would be shared later on. At this time, my wife Margaret used to do part-time teaching in Knockiandhu School on Monday afternoons and Norman's wife Greta was the Head Teacher there. After I came home from Leurbost School on the Monday following the fishing outing and when dinner was ready Margaret gave me a call and when I came to the table I was astounded to see two uncooked fish stomachs on my plate. I just stared at them and Margaret said: "Be sure your sins will find you out! Examine what's on your plate."

This I did and in each fish stomach I found a piece of blue plastic which put together read: 'Watson of Aberdeen'. It transpired that when Norman was cleaning his share of the catch he examined the contents of their stomachs as he was wont to do but which I seldom did. Without damaging the blueish stomachs of two of the haddock he realised what they contained! When I was in the Maths class in Glasgow University I heard of the Theory of Probability but fortunately I did not have to answer a question on it otherwise I don't think I would have passed my Maths degree examination! However, I will list the sequence of events and hopefully someone out there can calculate what the odds are that the blue labels should arrive at my dinner table!

1) Norman and I were fishing in Loch Erisort in approximately 11 fathoms of water towards the end of the ebb tide which was moving at about 2-3 knots.

2) We dropped two pieces of plastic overboard.

3) There were few fish caught until the tide turned; thereafter we were able to fill a standard herring basket with a variety of fish.

4) The catch was shared when we came ashore and when Norman was cleaning his share at home he noticed that the stomachs of two haddock had a blue tinge and by careful examination without damaging the stomachs he realised what was in them. Haddock are demersal fish — the question is, how far from Aite na Caillich were the plastic pieces when the haddock ate them.

5) I did not as a rule examine the stomach contents of fish when gutting them.

In 1959 the proprietor of Soval Estate, Mr W J Humbert, approached Mr John Buchanan, then Head Teacher of Balallan School and discussed with him the possibility of forming an Angling Association which would incorporate memebership of all residents on the Estate who wished to join. Mr Buchanan, a keen angler mooted this proposal and a steering committee consisting of Mr Buchanan as Chairman, myself as Secretary and Mr Donald Mackinnon, 43 Balallan as Treasurer was set up. A Constitution was formulated in consultation with Mr Humbert who granted us fishing rights on over 20 trout lochs. The Soval Angling Association is probably the only recreational organisation still extant without a lapse in the Soval Estate for almost 50 years.

In my younger days I often went fishing to Langavat on foot and on my own. Whenever the loch appeared I would start running – such was my eagerness to get there and my anticipation of a good day's fishing – I was seldom disappointed. In those days I would spend a whole day at the loch without seeing a single soul – what solitude and tranquillity – and I was never less alone than when alone. On one particular occasion, after experiencing a stormy day on my previous visit I found myself on the loch on what I considered an excellent fishing day and the Muse came along and the poem opposite called Langavat was the result.

I recall an occasion when Norman Mackenzie and I were fishing a Lewis loch in a boat. The practice was that we would take turns of half an hour each alternatively fishing and rowing. On a particularly good fishing day when it was my turn to fish I hooked 9 trout with three casts and Norman successfully netted the nine within the half hour. I will revise that account: on my first cast I hooked a trout and that trout hooked another and the two of them hooked a third trout! With my Sage rod – a birthday present from Margaret, my wife – I kept a steady pressure on the fish until at last they had played themselves out and I was able to draw them in line astern towards Norman who scooped them 'tail end Charlie' first into the net. (Pardon the mixture of Naval and Air Force metaphors!) The

Mi 'n seo gu tràth air creagan bàn
An cladach fiadhaich Langabhat
A ghaoth na deann tighinn thar nam beann
Le usbag luath neo-cheannsachail

An t-uisge mìn tighinn tro na glinn
S a'siabadh nuas na mòintichean
A' cheo a sguabadh thar nan cluan
S a'laigh' air gualainn Ròinebhail.

Na h-uillt le gàir a nuas am blàr
A'cireadh fraoich is coinnich ann:
Chan fhaod iad tàmh gus 'n ruig iad àit
'San sgaoil an treòir bh'air mòintich ac'

Na tuinn a'fàs ach gheibh iad bàs
Air clachan liòmht neo-thruacanta
An cìrein bàn gam frasadh àrd
'San loch gu lèir cho buaireasach.

Mo smuaintean luaineach 's mi fo ghruaim
Na speuran duaichnidh ' sìoladh orm
M'inntinn cuairtaicht ' gun dòigh fuasglaidh
Cha gheàrr an tuagh na neòil ud dhomh.

Mar eun tha 'n cuing cha toir mi taing
Don Fhreasdal chruaidh neo-chuimhneachail
Tha m'aigne mùcht' chan fhaigh mi saors'
Mo chridhe làn mi-thaingealachd.

Ach seall mi'n dràsd air leacan àrd
A 'ghrian a' deàrrsachd fialaidheachd
A ghaoth o dheas a' tighinn le teas
Is oiteag chneasd' nach fuaraich mi.

Na sgothan bàn a'seòladh àrd
Tro speuran maiseach mìn-cheothach
Na h-eòin len dàn 's mo chridhe làn
Macmeanmhuin 'se cho luaisgeanach.

Nach math an dràsd bhith 'n tac an àit
'San tàmh am bradan geur- shuileach
An dùil ri sgobadh bhon fhear ghobach
'Sa' faicinn ruith air driamlaich.

The following is a rough translation

Here I am on a white knoll
On the wild shores of Langavat
The wind in haste comes o'er the bens
With fast gusts uncontrollable.

The fine drizzle comes through the glens
Sweeping across the moors
The mist brushes over the landscape
And rests on the shoulder of Roineval.

The burns with a roar come down the moor
Combing the heather and moss there
They cannot rest till they reach the place
Where their moorland strength deserts them.

The waves are rising but they shall end
On polished merciless stones
Their white combs are splashing high
The loch is all so turbulent.

My thoughts are restless: I am so sad
The gloomy skies surround me
My mind is caught and there's no release
An axe can't cleave those clouds for me.

Like a bird in a cage I can't give thanks
To the hard forgetful Providence
My mind is choked – I can't feel free
My heart is full of thanklessness.

But watch me now on a high ledge
The sun shining bountifully
The wind from the south comes with heat
And a gentle zephyr that warms me.

The white clouds are sailing high
Through beautiful skies with fine mist
The birds sing their songs and my heart is full
My imagination is now at full swing.

Is it not now wonderful to be in this place
Where the sharp-eyed salmon lies -
Hoping for a tug from the one with the snout
And see the line running until its almost out

A good day's fishing with rods on Loch Erisort with Norman Mackenzie, Keose.

occasion was the one and only time both of us had such an experience but I give most of the credit to Norman because of the expertise and split-second timing he exhibited in his part of the operation!

I enjoyed many fishing trips with the late Edward Young, formerly Rector of The Nicolson Institute. To get a taste of our fishing adventures here is a piece by Eddie – entitled Angels and Ministers of Grace Defend Us – which appeared in the Stornoway Gazette on September 24, 1998.

" I understand there is a growing belief in the USA of the existence of personal guardian angels who pop up at moments of crisis and save their charges from death, disaster or simple inconvenience. It all seemed a bit mediaeval to me, but I am beginning to believe that John M has one.

Two years ago, in 'Per Ardua ad Argocat', I wrote of the miraculous deliverances out on the moor when his last vehicle broke down in inconvenient places but came triumphantly home after John committed GBH with a heavy hammer on its mechanics.

This year while we were fishing in North Uist, his summer Montego estate (it needs a rest in the winter to recover) suffered a collapsed exhaust far from any garage, but it was patched together by Jock Handyside of Stag Lodge, and survived the rest of the week.

In July, returning from a happy day at Lacasdale Lochs, the car gently came to rest on the wrong side of the Clisham as its alternator expired. The shades of night were falling fast, and the cold rain poured down. We decided that I should hitch a lift to Balallan and call out the cavalry (in this case, Willie, John's son-in-law). Two large and expensive cars (from Away?) passed us at speed, their drivers visibly flinching at the sight of two soaked and gesticulating tatterdemalions, but a kind former pupil with a fully occupied car stopped and took a message. Hardly had this car departed when we saw a huge low-loader coming from Harris. It drew to a halt with, miraculously, Willie at the wheel! I refuse to believe that this was simple coincidence. Anyway, we arrived in Balallan in some style!

Earlier this month, after I had received absolute assurances that the Argocat (a newer model) was in perfect working order, even to being forced to give it a practice turn of the ignition key (it started first time), the MD of STRAB Engineering and I reported to Balallan one morning for the long-awaited expedition to the interior, only to find a puzzled figure claiming, 'It started perfectly last night.' I left it to the experts who finally managed to start the engine by unorthodox means, unfortunately in reverse gear, leading to its ending in the 'allt' (the stream) after bouncing John into perfect VTOL mode.(Vertical Take Off and Landing)

Naturally, with the guardianship he enjoys, he made a perfect landing without discomfort on the padded seat. Margaret, having idly glanced out of the window just when her husband was at his highest trajectory, shuddered and went to make some restorative coffee. Asserting myself, I suggested it was guardian angel time and, this time summoned by earthly telephone, Willie rapidly appeared driving a mighty Shogun, delivered only the day before (significant?) and hauled the Argocat on to dry land. He also demonstrated simple emergency procedures for starting, involving bare wires, a screwdriver and an impressive shower of sparks. He politely declined my suggestion that he should follow us out to the loch in case of further trouble.

After the much needed coffee, we set out with all systems firing over the wettest moor I have ever seen and at speed. All went well until the track became a morass and the Argo became stuck and in danger of sinking. We unloaded everything except the driver, and stuffed heather under each wheel. Eventually we despaired, but refused to admit it. I looked in vain to the ridge behind us, but no Seventh Cavalry or even a low-loader appeared. We finally noticed a tiny spot of firmer ground behind one rear wheel, and unexpected success was achieved when we manhandled the Argo onto a little more of it and reversed out. None of us believed it would work, but miraculously it did.

Lewis was bang in the middle of a stationary depression; there was no wind; the rain poured down for most of the day; the midges were in great fettle; and the salmon we saw disporting themselves as we arrived went straight down and never showed again as we pushed the boat out. We managed two hard-won trout among us. As we started home we traversed an even wetter moor than on the way out, but we out-flanked the way-in bad bit only to hit a huge and impossible-to-avoid flooded area. Again we lightened the load and John M went at full speed over what looked like a grassy lake, on the principle that moving fast would prevent sinking. Miraculously (that word again), it worked, and as the MD and I stood applauding we discovered that we should have kept on moving too, and only with difficulty extracted ourselves and our wellies. But we had to slog through the stuff to catch up with the complacently angel-protected driver, reminiscent of my youthful days of wading through glutinous, strength-sapping eastern paddy fields in full infantry gear. The only thing missing was the pong.

After that, we were home – and wet! Amazingly, we all confessed that we had enjoyed a hilarious day. We had overcome seemingly impossible difficulties at moments of well-concealed despair, finally triumphing against the odds. Is this, however, merely the first onset of what psychologists will eventually describe as The Last of the Summer Wine Syndrome? Certainly, drenched and somewhat mud-stained, we all looked a bit like Compo at the end of the day, but a hot bath and a change of clothing removed the illusion – I think. We decided to do it again – next year.

For what became annual visits to North Uist in the 1990's, with accomm-odation courtesy of Dr John and Lorna Macleod, a triumvirate was formed when Roddy John Macleod, former Head of Mathematics in The Nicolson joined Eddie and myself. He was recruited for a variety of reasons; (a) his Herculean strength – he broke an oar the first time we were caught in a gale! (b) his complete selflessness when it was his turn to take the oars – e.g. once he took me downwind across a loch where he was sure fish would be lying and so they were – I caught a beautiful trout of nearly 2lbs and then despite my pleadings to take an oar on the way back against the wind he flatly refused. On reflection I'm not sure if this was a compliment! (c) his repertoire of bed-time stories was inexhaustible and both hilarious and exhilarating!

On our visits, we were very impressed with the hospitality of NUAC members and also of many others with special mention of the late Alice Macdonald who welcomed us on arrival with a cup of coffee and ensured that we did not have to leave the loch at any time to go shopping, and also George Macdonald, Factor of the Estate, who was most co-operative and helpful to ensure that we enjoyed our visits to North Uist. Our visits ended with the sad demise of Eddie in January 2005.

Happy fishers – above, Eddie Young, left, and myself
Below, Dr John Macleod of Lochmaddy is seen presenting Eddie with his life membership of North Uist Angling Club accompanied by myself and Roddy John, right.

A good catch from North Uist, taken by Eddie Young, R.J. 'Barts' Macleod and myself

The first trout I caught in North Uist

The picture on the right shows the teams from a football match at Goathill Park, Stornoway, between a Lewis Select XI and a Highland League Select XI – the Lewis team are in the dark jerseys and I am in the front centre with the ball at my feet. Lewis lost the match on July 28, 1950 in which I scored our only goal in the 4:1 defeat.

On demobilisation in 1947, I was still keen on football and I got my first games with Stornoway Rovers. Lochs at this time did not have a team in the League. I still remember the star player the Rovers had – Adam Macleod who seemed to have a magnetic attachment with the ball which no other human could sever!

I also played for Stornoway United under Duncan 'Waynes' leadership and I enjoyed those days tremendously especially the 'away' games when the repartee on the bus was superior to any comic show that was then available! In 1957 when I left United to play for Lochs who had then joined the League, I was presented with a most elegant trophy by United which I have always cherished.

I played for Lochs for a short time but on one occasion when we were playing Ness I found myself being outrun by a flying Niseach and I then decided to retire from playing League football.

However, I still enjoyed watching games and I can recollect some very amusing incidents I witnessed as a spectator. Back and Point were the main rivals in the Lewis League during the post-war years with both teams having eminent players – Stoodie, Hoddan and Kenny Staraidh played for Point and Back had stalwarts like Ginger Macleod and Dan Murray.

On one occasion when Lochs were playing at Back I happened to be standing beside Seoras Shoyan and Angus John Macleod was the linesman for Lochs (in those days linesmen were not supposed to be neutral!) Seoras in his enthusiasm supporting Back kept stepping over the line. Angus John resented this and stamped on Seoras' toes. This caused a furore and the Ref stopped the game. When the Ref asked Angus John for an explanation he replied "The crowd were invading the pitch!"

There was another amusing incident involving Point and Back. Point were playing in Back and many Point folk were cutting peats on the route the Point bus took on their way home. One of the peat cutters ran to the roadside, stopped the bus and asked for the score. 3-1 he was told but he omitted to ask for whom. Back had won! John Murdo Macmillan used to report games in these days but his suggested title "By Bayble streams they sat and wept" was not accepted!

During my time at Glasgow University I sometimes played football for the first team but not on a regular basis. While I was at Jordanhill Training College four Lewismen – Donald Macdonald (Joker); Calum Mackay (Sankey); Alex Macdonald (Marco) and I all played for the First Team. This was surely a unique occurrence to have four Lewismen playing at the same time in the Jordanhill Football Team – I was the odd man out as the other three were Siarachs from the Wild West!

The staff of Leurbost School in 1979 – from left, Murdo Morrison, Christine Macmillan, Art (d);Murdina Macleod, primary (d); Ishbel Montgomery, primary; John M Macleod, headteacher; Mairi Macleod, primary; Patricia Macleod, remedial; Kenneth D Smith, secondary (d); Peter Ross, piping instructor (d).

Chapter 9
Community co-operation and local customs

From my earliest memories there were facilities at 50 Balallan, which was my home until I got married in July 1953, for carrying out the various operations necessary for maintaining a healthy sheep-stock. It was my father who carried out the improvements after we came home from Port Glasgow and they included a dipping-tank and dripper; the latter ensured that surplus dip in the wool of the sheep after they had their bath would flow back into the tank – waste not, want not!

He also converted the ruins of a bothy which lay alongside the dipping facilities into a two compartment fank, which made up a complex that was simple but effective. Most of the crofters from No.45 Balallan to No.55 made use of them on a particular day which was communally agreed upon. However, my grandfather had the power of veto after consulting Donald Macmillan next door – Donald of the White Horse who probably saved my life when I had measles! I mentioned before that he was a noted weather forecaster whose predictions were miraculously accurate. Every evening before he retired to bed he would go outside and survey the heavens, making mental notes of signs by which he was able to predict the weather for at least twenty four hours ahead.

Sheep were an important item in the economy of Lewis after World War 1 and still are although not to the same extent. In those days there were not many local wage-earners apart from weavers and road-workers in the Lochs area. During Lord Leverhulme's years as owner of Lewis he offered to change the island into an industrial area largely based on fishing and fish-processing. This episode in the history of Lewis is already well documented and the end result was that Lewis continued to exist mainly on an agricultural economy rather than on an industrial one. After Lord Leverhulme left for Harris, the rural community passed through a period of want and poverty but as happened in both world wars and their aftermaths they were able to survive due to the existing assets prevailing which were outwith the reach of most city dwellers.

1.   Food: most households had hens, hence no shortage of eggs.

2.   Most crofts would yield at least potatoes, oats and vegetables.

3.   Fuel in the form of peat was in abundance and by community co-operation it could be secured in season. It was customary for fit and young men

Sheep Dipping at 50 Balallan – Pictured right to left: Sophie Macleod and her mother Christina Macleod 50 Balallan; Dolly Maclean and John Angus 51 Balallan; Alistair Nicolson 47 Balallan; Johnnie Nicolson 45 Balallan; George Mackenzie 55 Balallan; Roddy Macleod 50 Balallan; James Montgomery 58 Balallan; Murdo Mackenzie 54 Balallan; Dolly Macdonald 52 Balallan; Ian Martin Stornoway

to cut peats for a widow in their neighbourhood.

4.   Fish was to be found in abundance in Loch Erisort and elsewhere around Lewis while the 3-mile limit for trawlers still prevailed. Not only could crofters still enjoy a leisurely evening catching fish for domestic use but they could also provide sustenance to the elderly and infirm neighbours among whom a share of the bounty was invariably distributed.

5.   Most able-bodied crofters had two cows so that by manipulating their calving times the households always had a supply of milk all the year round.

6.   As for a meat supply, it was customary to kill a few wedders usually in October and November when they were in their prime condition. In those days there were no freezers and the methods of meat preservation varied:- (a) Some were eaten fresh and that was the end of that! (b) Some were salted and stored in barrels. There were no hydrometers in the crofters' houses but they devised their own method to determine the salinity required to cure meat properly. A tub was half-filled with water and coarse salt was added to the water gradually. A raw potato was cleaned and inserted in the tub. As more and more salt was slowly applied, the potato eventually floated to the surface! Why bother with a BSc degree when the bodachs of Balallan knew it all! The salinity of the water

was perfect and the meat was submerged in it for a specific time. In the thatched houses some of the meat was hung in the room where the fire was – aig an teine – and by spring-time it would be thoroughly peat-smoked and it was called 'feòil-rèisg'. Very often a widow in the neighbourhood would be given a share.

When slaughtering took place it was done in as humane a way as possible without any sanctimonious sanctions from outside 'bodies'. At an early age I was introduced to the operation and I served a useful function. I was provided with a clean enamel pail in which a handful of salt had been placed and when the blood poured into the pail I stirred it vigorously with a ladle to prevent it from coagulating; the blood was later used for making black puddings. When my father had skinned the animal he would extract the various organs in a prescribed sequence and tell me the Gaelic and English names:

1. Maodal – stomach – retained and cleaned to make 'maragan' – puddings.

2. An Adha – the liver – retained if pure. Attached to the liver was the gall-bladder – Dulmasg. This was given to dogs suffering from distemper and it cured them!

3. An Cridhe – the heart – retained.

4. Dubhagan – kidneys – retained.

5. Ròmhsan – the tail (delicious when singed and roasted!)

6. An Aotraman – bladder – dispensed with.

7. Sgamhain – lungs – dispensed with.

8. Staoig an amadain – pancreas – dispensed with

9. Caisean-uchd – the breast-strip, difficult to remove; used at Oidhche Challuinn, Hogmanay, 'caisean-uchd nam mo phòcaid, 's math an treòir a thig bhon fhear ud' – part of Duan na Calluinn. 'a breast-strip in my pocket, great is the strength that emanates from that one.' A sheep's ròmhsan is delicious but a deer's ròmhsan is superb!

My father, ex-shipwright on the Clyde, used to be called to Eishken to repair boats that had sustained damage during the fishing season. He used to stay there during the week and came home at the weekends. My grandfather, who had spent most of his working life at Eishken Estate, asked him what was happening to the tails of the deer that had been shot. When my father told him that they were thrown away, he gasped with astonishment and told him to salvage as many as he could.

The following Saturday my father arrived with about half a dozen deer tails in his pockets. I never forgot the gleam of joy in my grandfather's eyes when he saw the bonanza in front of him. He immediately took command and said to my mother in Gaelic "Ciorstaidh, bring me all the grease-paper you have and also some brown paper." With the sheep shears he clipped most of the hair off

the tails and singed the stubble left, scraping the tails with a knife until they were
as smooth as a baby's bottom! First of all, he wrapped them in the grease-paper
and then in copious layers of brown paper. We had a range in the room – a grate
where the peats were placed and beneath the grate was a space for the ashes. My
grandfather inserted the packages deeply into the the ashes and then he poked
the roaring peat fire furiously and red-hot embers fell on top of the ashes which
caused the packages to sizzle with a mouth-watering sound which excited me no
end. However, the Commander-in-Chief was now in full charge and no-one
would dare make a move except under orders! An order by him addressed to my
mother was quickly obeyed and an ashet arrived with due alacrity. He then
extracted parcel after parcel of charred brown paper – their contents still sizzling
and placed them gingerly into the ashet with the long tongs that were always an
adjunct to the hearth in those days.

Like the phoenix of old, the tails of the 'Monarchs of the Glen' rose from
the ashes at 50 Balallan that evening and as I watched with appreciation and
anticipation, like the 'ranks of Tuscany' on another famous occasion, I could
'scarce forbear to cheer.' By this time not only was my mouth watering it was
positively salivating and I looked at my grandfather with pleading eyes but he
said to me, 'Biodh foighidinn agad, Iain, mus loisg thu do theangha' (Have
patience, John, in case you burn your tongue) In later years I realised he was
teaching me a salutary lesson in his own inimitable way.

Another delicacy that we had the good fortune to enjoy in those days was the
singed head of a wedder. The preparation was time consuming but well worth
the effort when the finished article appeared in the middle of the table on a large
platter; and we must not forget the delicious, appetizing but perhaps soporific
plates of soup that served as starters. To prepare the singed head the procedure
was as follows:-

First of all, the wool had to be clipped off the head with shears and then by
holding each horn in turn the head was held in the flames of a prepared fire until
all the wool was singed off. In the meantime iron bars were placed in the fire
until they were white-hot and then holding them in turn with a damp sack they
were rubbed against the face of the wedder until it became absolutely smooth.
Then the eyes were pierced with a knife and the jelly rubbed onto the skin. After
that the head was cut longitudinally, the horns cut off and the brains extracted:
this was also rubbed on the wedder's face and then scraped off with a large knife.
This resulted in cleaning the face thoroughly of charcoal and also eliminating
any smell of singeing. The ears were cut off before the singeing began.

I feel thankful that we always had Black-faced sheep with horns as I hate to
think about the problems that would be involved should we have had Cheviot
sheep with no horns! When the process was finished the head would be given a
thorough wash and then left overnight to soak in a container of saline water.

At that time people had great faith in local medication as a cure for different ailments and here are several that come to mind :-

Corn on Sole of Foot: Select a small limpet, boil it and remove contents; mix Archangel tar and oatmeal and insert mixture in shell. Place shell over corn and wind bandage round shell and foot. After a couple of days remove bandage and shell and extract corn.

Lus nan Laogh: (For blood impurities causing boils, pimples and varicose ulcers) 'Lus nan Laogh' is translated as 'saxifrage' by Edward Dwelly but in Lewis it is known as 'bog-bean' and is a trefoil plant usually found growing in bogs and streams alongside water lilies. The easy way to collect it is to attach a long handle to a sharpened sickle and cut it near the bottom, as the stems contain most of the juice. It will float to the surface and it can be pulled to the bank with a rake. Clean thoroughly by scrubbing in cold water, cut stems into convenient lengths, say 4-6 inches and insert together with leaves into largest pan available. Cover the 'lus' with boiling water, bring pan to the boil then let it simmer (not boil) for 6 to 8 hours. When it is ready sieve through a sterilised cloth into a sterilised jug and then into sterilised bottles.

King's Evil – Scrofula: The seventh son (or daughter) washed their hands in water in which a silver sixpence (old currency) had been immersed. The water was then applied to the affected glands to effect a cure.

Lumbago: A person suffering from this painful ailment would lie face down on the floor and a person who had a breech birth would stand on the ailing person's back and thus be cured.

Curing a Stye: The afflicted person would sit and stare straight ahead while the healer – usually a lady – would sit opposite with a darning needle which she would bring close up to the eye with the sharp point forward and then bring it back while incanting in Gaelic "Why should there be one without two? Why should there be two without three? right up to nine and then backwards; "Why should there be nine without eight, etc", ending with "Why should there be one without any?"

In addition many customs and superstitions also abounded

CAITHRIS NA H-OIDHCHE – night long courting in the girls' home was a time honoured institution and it probably came about because of the lack of organised venues where 'boy meets girl' was in vogue. When a couple 'clicked' the next step towards matrimony was the:-

RÈITEACH: (The Betrothal) About three weeks before the proposed marriage, the prospective groom and his best man would go to the bride's home and ask her father for his daughter's hand. There was a Gaelic love song supposedly composed by the bride-to-be: 'O is fhada leam gus an tig thu le do phigidh air do ghualain!' I long until you arrive with your pitcher on your shoulder! The pitcher of course would be full of whisky and was meant to lubricate the tongue of the bride's father!

Meantime a few girls would be in the 'cùlaist', the upper room, and they appeared one by one, the bride-to-be coming last. As each one appeared the prospective father-in- law would ask his prospective son-in-law "What about this one?"The groom-to-be would look her over carefully and have to give a valid excuse for rejecting each one e.g. "She hasn't got child bearing hips!"The next one perhaps did not have a back suitable for carrying a creel of peats, etc, etc. However, when the betrothed appeared the groom would extol her virtues and her beauty and embrace her lovingly! He would then ask her father for her hand, which was always granted. Thereafter a good time would be had by all!

The wedding would follow within a short time -

BANAIS (Wedding) In the olden days this invariably took place in the bride's home: pre-wedding arrangements for catering were always carried out there with the help of willing neighbours. The poultry population in the area was drastically reduced at the time of weddings and the ladies who had donated a hen, and there were many of them, would attend an assembly of hen-pluckers mutually arranged prior to the wedding night. This would be an evening of hard work and hilarity but hard work is easier when the repartee and humour are of a high standard, and again 'many hands make light work'. The guests would gather at the bridal home and sit in relays at a table where a sumptuous meal was always provided. At the end of each sitting someone at the table would be asked to propose a toast to the bridal couple. There was always someone who could do that and usually the toast ended "Slàinte nan daoin' òga agus slàinte na waitearan!" – Good health to the young couple and also to the waitresses! In the meantime a dance would be in progress in a barn or other suitable building with lanterns for lighting – it was in 1954 that electricity was introduced in our area.

BANAIS TAIGHE (House Wedding): If the bride belonged to a village a long distance away from the groom's home a celebration was arranged the following evening in the groom's home and it was at a 'Banais Taighe' that I first 'clicked' with Margaret. Her next door neighbour, Angus Morrison, was a cousin of mine and we both got an invitation to the 'Banais Taighe.'

That evening in July 1950 I happened to be playing football for a Lewis Select team against a Highland League Select. We were beaten 4-1 but I scored the one goal for Lewis and when I arrived at the Wedding Dance in Balallan School I felt a little big-headed; so much that I invited Margaret to go out for a breather! She agreed and that was the beginning of a romance that has lasted over 58 years and is still going strong! We decided to get married on the 14th of July 1953 but Margaret claims that I never proposed to her and come to think of it, she is probably right! However, as we had been courting for two years and the 'Rèiteach' tradition had died out, no-one was surprised when we announced the

Above, the wedding party of John M. Macleod and Margaret M. Maciver in Kinloch Church on July 14, 1953 and below, with the their immediate family, at their Golden Wedding anniversary at Tulloch Castle in Dingwall

date of the wedding. When we began to make a list of the wedding guests, I was astonished when Margaret revealed that she had 47 first cousins and I had a few myself! Neither the Caberfeidh nor the Seaforth Hotels had been built at this time and when we contacted all the other hotels in Stornoway we discovered that 40 guests was the maximum any of them could cater for.

Someone had a brainwave and so we approached the Masonic Hall in Stornway and enquired if they would hire the hall to us on 14th July and the number of guests that could be accommodated. We were told that the hall could hold 120 guests but they could not do the catering. As none of the hotels would cater either, because we had by-passed them there was only one thing to do – call in the Balallan East End Ladies Brigade and organise the preparation of the food at 15a Balallan. This was done under the direction of Margaret and her late sister Iana. Having the food prepared in good time, it was safely transported to Stornoway in the morning by a good neighbour, Malcolm Macleod, 13 Balallan in his large van and not a drop of the soup was spilt! Soon afterwards Margaret and I tied the matrimonial knot in Kinloch Church of Scotland and it is still as tight as ever.

MÀIREAD

Bha do chuailean bàn bachallach
A chiad latha thachair sinn;
Is bha do dheudan mar na seudan
Geal mar chanach brèagha na
macharach.

Cha b'e do chuailean na do dheudan
A mhàin a tharruing mise fagaisg ort
Ach an saighead chuir thu trom chridhe
A dh'èignich orm èirigh is laighe leat.

Ar leam nach robh a riamh' sa'
chruinne-cè
Te bhòidheach de do shamhail-sa
Oir chuir thu mo chridhe-sa ruith na
leum
A h-uile uair a dh'amhaircinn ort.

Ged bha te bhòidheach ann an Troy
A dh'aobhraich mòran an-shocair
Is beag a shaoilinn dhith rim thaobh
An tac ri Màiread shubhailceach.

Rough Translation

Your locks were fair and curly,
The first day that we met;
And your teeth were like jewels,
White as meadow-sedge.

It was neither your locks nor your teeth
Alone that drew me to you so close
But it was the arrow with which you pierced my heart
That brought me into your sweet embrace.

Me thinks that ne'er in the whole creation,
Was there one so beautiful and true,
Because you set my heart a-racing,
Every time I gazed at you.

Although in Troy there was a beauty,
Who caused so much unrest,
Little would I think of her beside me
Compared to virtuous Margaret

Chapter 10

The Whales of Balallan

A major incident occurred in the community in the autumn of 1934. A pal, Norman Mackenzie 57 Balallan and I were creeping like snails unwillingly back to school at lunch-time when we noticed that an unusual activity was taking place in the 'Struth' – the narrows in Loch Erisort between Cleitir to the south and the crofts adjacent to the school in the north. We immediately decided to go and investigate, and bare-footed as we were we soon arrived at the scene of action. On arrival we were amazed to see that the waters of the 'Struth' were red. It was slack-tide (liogann) and a pod of whales was being attacked by the weaponry of Balallan ranging from scythes, which cut off their fins – thus the blood, to graips (iron dung forks) which were not too effective, World War One rifles and other weaponry of which the Germans had been relieved.

There were plenty of WW1 veterans present and one of them must have taken command and the strategic plan evolved was to slip a long rope with a running noose on it over the tail of a whale and then row furiously for dry land where the shore brigade would take over and drag the unfortunate mammal ashore. If the coaches of the Oxford and Cambridge boat races had been present I am sure they would have been impressed. In all battles there are always casualties and in this encounter one crofter, while trying to fit a noose over the tail of a whale, received a violent swipe from the said tail and landed in the water among the whales – just as well they were not sharks! Fortunately it was not a meaningless slaughter as the blubber was removed from the captured whales and melted in cauldrons and used for various purposes, eg to mix with animal feed giving calves in Balallan a lustrous shining coat; to pour some on the backs of sheep to waterproof them during the winter and some people even used it as an embrocation for arthritic joints! Some critics in South Lochs who had no faith in the seafaring qualities of the Balallan folk wrote a satirical poem in Gaelic decrying the stupidity of the whales in searching refuge at the inner end of Loch Erisort.

Here is a rough translation

Mucan Mara Bhailailein

Se mucan gun chiall chuir cùl ri'n dachaidh
Air aodann mharail a' chuain
Nuair chuir iad an cùrs air bàgh Bhailailein
'Se am bàs a bh'aca mar dhuais

The Whales of Balallan

It was senseless whales that forsook their dwelling
On the briny face of the ocean
When they set their course on Balallan Bay
Death was to be their portion

'Se aon a thàrr gu sàl air ais dhiubh
Chaidh càch a chlachadh gun truas
Bha balaich an àit' nam màl a' feannadh
Gu tràth air madainn Di-luain.

It was only one that managed to escape
The rest were stoned without mercy
The local lads were busy flensing
Early on Monday morn.

Dh'obraich iad cruaidh ri fuachd na maidne
Gu faigheadh iad dhachaidh an t-saill
Bha praisean le sùrd ri taobh gach deathach
Ri taobh gach abhainn is allt
A brùdhadh gu smeuradh sùgh a' bheathaich
Thug Ionah caithris 'na broinn
'Sa dhìobhair i'n àrd air tràigh a' bhaile
Bha gràin aig air a dhol ann.

They laboured hard in the morning cold
In order to salvage the blubber
Beside each fire were bubbling pots
Beside each river and stream
For smearing the sheep with the oil of the creature
Which Jonah spent time inside
But was vomited up on the shore of the city
That he dreaded to visit.

'Sa mhadainn Di-màirt bha fàileadh damait
Gu h-àrd air mullach nam beann
Gun dh'fhairich na fèidh iad fèin an saf
A bha 'g èirigh mach as a' ghleann
Tharraing iad ceum le leum is osann
'Se 'n èiginn a chumadh iad ann
 Chan itheadh iad beum de'n fheur gu ruigeadh
Iad slèibhtean Ùisinis thall.

On Tuesday morn there was a vile odour high on the tops of the bens
The deer themselves detected the smell
That was rising out of the glens
Off they set with a leap and a sigh
Desperation alone would keep them there
They wouldn't eat a bite of grass
Till they reached the slopes of Usinis beyond.

'S gu dè thug air ainmhidhean garbh na mara
Cur cùl ri'n dachaidhean fhèin
Air tòir teachd-an-tìr ri crìch a' chladaich
An sgìr a'bhradain san fhèidh?
'S ann stiùir iad an cùrs le ùidh air camus
Bhiodh cùilteach falaichte rèidh
'Sam biodh iad le rian fo dhìon nam fearaibh
Nach trialladh mara chum èisg.

Whatever made the great creatures of the sea
Abandon their own abodes
Looking for a livelihood by the edge of the shores
In the land of the salmon and deer
They steered their course intent on a bay
That would be remote, hidden and smooth
Where they would be safe and sheltered by the Protection of the lads who would never go fishing in the sea.

Chan fhaigheadh iad àit bu shàbhailt leotha
Na bàgh Bhailailein is Cheòis
Fìor nàmhaid an èisg no creutair mara
Cha b'e bha 'm balaich a' chlò
Cha chàradh iad lìon, cha rèileadh iad dubhan
Cha bhiadhadh duin' ac' lion-mòr
Ach leithid a' mhìolachd riamh cha d' rinneadh
Air iasg a bheannaich an òb.

They couldn't get a place that was safer for them
Than the Bays of Balallan and Keose
The boys of the tweed were never the foes
Of any fish or sea creature.
They couldn't mend a net or set up a hook
None of them could bait a long line
But never was such havoc meted out
To fish that blessed the bays.

Chapter 11

The Park Deer Raid

Some people may consider the word 'Clearance' to mean the eviction of men, women and children overseas but there is a totally different interpretation of the word in the context of forcibly removing people from their homes to other areas in their immediate environment or to areas within the Island of Lewis.

In a letter written to the 'Stornoway Gazette' by the late Donald Mackay, Kershader he reveals that those giving evidence to the Napier Commission prior to the passing of the Crofters Act of 1886 gave varying figures for the number of townships cleared in Park from the beginning of the 19th Century – 28, 30, 45. Donald himself gave a list of 34 townships 'desolated' as he puts it during that period and he states that the list is not necessarily complete. The list is as follows: -

1. Leumrabhagh	13. Bunchorchabig	25. Gleann Claidh
2. Oronsaidh	14. Brollum	26. Sgealadal Mhòr
3. Stiòmrabhagh	15. Ceann Chriònaig	27. Ach-an-Taib
4. Isginn	16. Gilmicpharg	28. Caolas nan Eilein
5. Gearraidh Raisdeal	17. Bhalamus Beag	29. Brinigeil
6. Ceann-tigh-shealg	18. Bhalamus Mòr	30. Sromos
7. Gearraidh Reasaidh	19. Bàgh	31. Ceann-a-Carragh
8. Ailteinish	20. Ceann Bhaighmhoir	32. Seaforth
9. Buthnish	21. Chulebreac	33. Shieldinish
10. Molchadha-Gearraidh	22. Ceannamhuir	34. Cleiteir
11. Mol Truisg	23. Sgealadal Bheag	
12. Smuaisebhig	24. Airidh Dhòmhnuill Chaim	

In no way can these internal evictions be tolerated for anything but what they were and that was the forcible removal of law-abiding people from their homes to make way for sheep and deer which would satisfy the whims and caprices of sport-loving and avaricious potentates from the South.

Some of my own ancestors suffered thereby. My great grandfather Angus Smith was moved from Brinigeil in Park to Cleitir and thence to Balallan. In those days roofing timber was at a premium in Lewis because of the lack of forests in the Island. Therefore it is said that my great grandfather carried the roofing timber at Brinigeil all the way to Cleitir, no mean performance.

The village of Crossbost in North Lochs originally emanated from people evicted from South Lochs who had been driven out of their homes by the landowners who did not seem to worry about the consequences of their cruel and inhumane behaviour. However, in 1887 the Park Deer Raid may have taught the oppressors a salutary lesson when the Courts of Law failed to support their dictatorial and undemocratic attitude to the downtrodden indigenous population.

There was another subtle type of population clearance at the start of the 20th century which emanated from Central Government. Despite the fact that Britain was wealthy, as was proven during World War One when millions of pounds were expended in creating a bloodbath in Europe, the economic situation in Lewis was catastrophic. The result was that many young lads from Lewis with initiative left their native land to find employment overseas. The majority from Lewis made for South America where many of them settled and found employment in Patagonia, Tierra del Fuego, Peru, etc. Three of my uncles were among them – two on my mother's side, John and Kenneth and one on my father's side, Angus and they are all buried there far from their kith and kin.

None of them ever came home and only Kenneth married and left descendants. While on a world tour recently one of my grand-daughters, Jennifer traced and visited a granddaughter of Kenneth and her family in Buenos Aires. On Friday evening they all went out for a meal and photographs were taken. Next morning our daughter Helen, Jennifer's mother received a copy of the group in Laxay, Isle of Lewis "The old order changeth yielding place to new!" A first cousin of my wife Margaret, Murdo Macleod, 25 Balallan, came back home on holiday from Patagonia in the Sixties and he told us that when he first went out to Patagonia there were 27 men from Balallan there and many others from different parts of Lewis.

Smuaintean an Taca Teine Dealain

Tha siantan agus gèile an duine dhuibh a-muigh ach tha sìth agus sàmhchair a-staigh agus nach math sin! Tha mise 'n seo gu dòigheil mu choinneamh an teine – chan e teine mòr mònach ann am meadhan an làir ach teine dealain; cumaidh e mi blàth ach chan eil e gun uireasbhaidh. Chan eil lasraichean na mònach a' leum 's a' cur nan car dhiùbh mum choinneamh, a' dùsgadh mo mhac-meanmhainn mar a thachradh an linn mo sheanair.

Cha leig mise leas a dhol dhan chuil-mhònach a' leasachadh mo theine-sa – putaidh mi putan beag dubh gu dearg is bidh dearg-theine dealain agam; is gheibh mi teas no blàths mar is toigh leam, agus dathadh bho Bhòrd an Dealain!

Dh'fheumadh mo sheanair a dhol dhan a' pholl-mhònach leis an spaid bhig is bhiodh e 'na fhallas a' rùsgadh a' phuill 's dòcha ri latha gailleann. Thigeadh latha loinnearach is bhuaineadh e fàd as dèidh fòid; thigeadh latha grianach is rudhadh e gach fàd; thigeadh latha freagarrach airson na mònach a thoirt dhachaidh is stèidheadh e cruach shnasail chuimir ann an tac an doruis, is leigeadh e anail is osann-cinnteach gu robh connadh-Geamhraidh ri làimh dha fhèin 's dha chuid leannan.

Ma bhios acras orm-se 's dòcha gun can mi ri Màiread, 'Dè th'anns an reothadair?'

'Tha feòil is iasg gu leòr is eile' canaidh ise, Na biodh iomnaidh ort, cha bhi an t-acras ort ann an Dùbhlachd garbh a'Gheamhraidh no ann an laithean caol an Earraich.'

Cha b'ann mar sin bu nòs. Bha mult no dhà aig mo sheanair is mharbhadh e feadhainn san Fhoghar; bha sgian aige le faobhar mar an lanns is cha robh riaghailtean a' Mhargaidh Eòrpaich ann. Dheidheadh cuid den fheòil ithe ùr is an còrr dheidheadh dhan bharaille; dheidheadh cuid air an t-sìoman is e air a dheagh shailleadh; chanadh iad feòil-rèisg ri seo is abair annas nuair a thigeadh caoilead an Earraich is gun càil a' tighean as an talamh.

Cha robh talamh gu leòir aca airson feumalachd gach duine is chuir iad tagraidhean gu Cailleach NicMhathain aig an robh còir air an Eilean . Cha do rinn ise fiù 's am freagart: dè bh'annta ach tràillean gun fheum – na fèidh a b'fheàrr a dhèanadh feum den talamh.

Mar sin 'sa bhliadhna ochd deug ceithir fichead 'sa seachd chaidh cùim a chur an òrdugh le MacRath 'na àrd-cheannard, is rinn muinntir nan Loch air a' Phàirc is leag iad iomadh fiadh gu talamh. Nuair a ràinig iad Airgh Dhòmhnaill Chaim 's iomadh broinn a bha falamh gus na ròsd iad damh donn agus a dh'ith iad an sàth nuair a dh'iarr bodach còir beannachd.

And this is my rough translation

Thoughts Beside an Electric Fire

There is a downpour and a raging gale outside but there is peace and quiet inside and that is good. I am here in good fettle in front of the fire – not a peat fire in the middle of the floor, but an electric fire; it will keep me warm but it is not without disadvantages. The peat fire flames are not flickering and leaping before me wakening my imagination as they would in my grandfather's time.

I do not have to go to the peat store to brighten my fire – I will push a black button to red and I will have a red hot electric fire and I can get warmth and heat as I wish – and a scorching from the Electricity Board!

My grandfather would have to go to the peat bank with his spade and he would be sweating turfing the banks perhaps on a stormy day. A bright day would come and he would cut the bank peat after peat; a sunny day would come and he would lift them; a suitable day would come for carting them home and he would build an elegant, handsome stack near the door – and he would rest and sigh – satisfied that there was an adequate winter's supply of fuel available for himself and his loved ones.

If I am hungry perhaps I will say to Margaret: "What's in the freeze?"

"Meat and fish and plenty more" she will reply. "Don't worry, you will not go hungry during the dark days of winter nor the lean days of spring."

That is not how things were. My grandfather had some sheep and he would kill some wedders in the autumn. He had a razor-sharp knife and the rules and regulations of the Common Market did not exist. Some of the meat would be eaten fresh, some would be salted in a barrel and some well-salted would be suspended on hooks in the house and smoked and what a treat especially in the spring when produce was scarce.

The crofters did not have enough land for their requirements and so they appealed to Lady Matheson, the proprietrix, for more but she did not deign to reply. What were they but useless slaves – the deer would make better use of the ground.

Therefore in the year 1887 a plot was hatched under the command of Donald Macrae, Headmaster of Balallan School, and the Lochies made for Park and many a deer was shot. When they reached Dòmhnull Cam's shieling many a stomach was empty until they roasted a stag and had their fill after a kind old man had asked a blessing.

****

In the 1980's the late Angus 'Ease' Macleod decided that the struggle for better conditions about a century before by crofters should be recognised by the erection of memorials in the four areas of Lewis where direct action took place; Bernera, Lochs, Point and Back. A committee was formed consisting initially of a representative from each of those four areas and later other members were added. The organisation was known as Cuimhneachain nan Gaisgeach (Memorials to the Heroes) and the Chairman and Vice-Chairman were Angus Macleod and myself respectively. We worked under the auspices of the Lewis Council of Social Service (Voluntary Action Lewis now) and invaluable help was provided by the Director, Alasdair Nicholson; the Treasurer, Matt Bruce; and the ever obliging Secretary, Catherine. However, before matters really got under way Bernera withdrew from Cuimhneachain nan Gaisgeach and built a cairn of their own.

The three remaining areas were fortunate in obtaining funding from various bodies – the first being the Gulbenkian Foundation. Furthermore Will Maclean, the world-renowned architect offered his services gratis to design the three cairns and they are indeed magnificent structures, all commanding attention on their respective sites. Jim Crawford, the expert stone-mason involved, deserves great commendation for the excellence and expertise so evident in the construction of the three cairns.

The Pairc Cairn has entrances to it depicting the three districts that participated in the raid – South Lochs, Kinloch and North Lochs. A stair inside the Cairn leads to the top where an excellent view of the surrounding countryside can be enjoyed and which was beautiful and sunny on opening day. A large concourse of people led by pipers marched from Balallan School for about half a mile towards the Cairn near the Eishken road end; transport was provided for the rest of the way. The ceremony performed there enacted to a certain extent that which was performed at Airigh Dhòmhnaill Chaim on the night of the feast.

On the opening day of the Cairn – 24 May 1994 – I addressed the assembled company as follows (others also spoke)

"To the south of where we are standing here there lies the vast private estate of Park where many crofters at one time resided. Unfortunately, during the third and fourth decades of last century many of them were evicted – those of Isginn in 1833 and those of Orinsay and Shieldinish five years afterwards and in 1841 the same fate befell the crofters of Lemreway. All in all, sixty crofters were routed from Park.

Between 1883 and 1886 no-one could be found to rent Park and many Lochs people sent requests to the then proprietrix, Lady Matheson, asking for parts of Park on rent to alleviate their lot; she did not deign to answer them. However, in 1886 tenants were found for Park – Mr and Mrs Joseph Platt – and shortly after this the Rev. Donald MacCallum who was minister at Keose and a stalwart in the fight for Land Law Reform wrote a Gaelic poem of fourteen verses slating Mr Platt. The first verse roughly translated went like this:-

"I rule as far as I can see"

Said Bodach Isginn, "over moor and ben"

And that he spoke the truth has broken my heart

And he has left the land trembling with cold.

Another stalwart Land Leaguer came as Headmaster to Balallan School in January 1887. He was Donald Macrae, a native of Kyle of Lochalsh, and he soon proved to be a friend of the crofters. He organised meetings in Balallan School to discuss means and methods to alleviate the poverty and hardship prevalent at the time. Those meetings usually opened with prayer and the singing of verses from a Gaelic Psalm, something that we are emulating today.

Eventually Tuesday 22 November was chosen as the day when a well-

John M Macleod at the opening of the Pairc Raiders Memorial with Angus 'Ease' Macleod behind him.

publicised onslaught on the deer in Park should be undertaken. Mr Platt was out-with the island at the time but Mrs Platt; Murdo Macrae, Head Keeper of the estate; Farquhar Macrae, Game Keeper at Seaforth Head and some ghillies met the raiders at Seaforth Head. Mrs Platt tried to remonstrate with the raiders but they marched past muttering "No English, my lady". Murdo Macrae shouted in Gaelic, "Who's at your head?""Our bonnets" replied Seonaidh 'an Oig from Cromore. Macrae then said, "In God's name have you gone mad?" He could hardly believe his eyes!

The raiders entered Park in the then army formation of four abreast and soon the campaign was organised in detail. Around mid-day Sandy Macfarlane from Marvig along with a group of crofters met Douglas Thorneycroft, Mrs Platt's youngest brother at Loch Brollum. He and his ghillies had come ashore and engaged in conversation with the crofters who told him the reason for their presence. One of the ghillies opened a hamper of food they had with them. "For goodness sake, won't you share that food amongst us all" said Sandy Macfarlane. This was done on the orders of Douglas Thorneycroft and a dram was also offered to the crofters.

On Tuesday evening some of the deer were skinned and cut up and prepared for cooking but one stag was left whole and roasted at Airigh Dhomhnaill Chaim, opposite Airidhbhruaich where a camp had been set up in the shape of the letter 'L' with sails and cabers. It was a beautiful frosty night without a cloud in the sky, the stars shining brightly, Mòr Monadh and Sìthean an Airgid before them, Loch Seaforth behind them as calm as a mill-pond and reflecting the moonlight as from a river.

On Tuesday evening two reporters from Stornoway, John Macpherson and John Mackenzie persuaded Donald Macrae to take them to the camp-site. They were ferried across from Airidhbhruaich and when they approached the camp they were challenged. Donald Macrae spoke up and they received a hearty welcome. Some of those in the camp were engaged in conversation and some were singing songs – Duncan Ban Macintyre's amongst them. Donald Macrae, who was an astute individual made sure he did not go beyond the High Water Mark – thus in legal terms he did not set foot in Park.

On Wednesday morning the crofters sallied forth before daybreak and the slaughter of the deer continued. How many were killed is a matter of conjecture – something like the claims made by both sides in the last war – but it can be safely said that the number claimed by Mr Brankner, who owned Aline Estate at the time was a gross under estimate; he claimed two deer were killed!

On Wednesday evening Superintendent James Gordon and Sheriff Fraser met a group of crofter-hunters at Ruadh Chleit and the Sheriff asked the crofters to go home. They refused to do so and thereupon the Sheriff read the Riot Act explaining its significance in Gaelic as most of the crofters were non-English speaking. The Sheriff was a fluent Gaelic speaker and the crofters then explained to him that the reason for the raid was the dire state of poverty due to landlord oppression which they suffered. The Sheriff listened to them attentively and then the crofters left for home.

Due to publicity most of the national newspapers sided with the crofters but the 'Scotsman' took a firm stance against them. It advocated that it was high time that the people of Lochs were brought under the firm hand of the law. That was exactly what the authorities intended to do. Eighty soldiers of the Royal Scots under the command of a Captain Farquarson, were dispatched to Lewis from Maryhill Barracks in Glasgow and HMS Ajax was ordered to sail to Stornoway from Greenock with a detachment of Marines on board. She got as far as Ardnamurchan Point where her rudder was broken in a gale and she had to be ignominiously towed back to port – what a furore the Lochs crofters had caused! There were many exciting events in the Park Deer Raid but despite the military and naval sabre-rattling there was no direct confrontation between the crofters and the armed forces.

In the end six of the leaders were arrested and brought to trial in Edinburgh where they were charged, inter alia, with rioting. They were: Donald Macrae, Roderick Mackenzie, Murdo Macdonald from Balallan, John Matheson from Gravir, Malcolm Mackenzie and Donald Macmillan from Crossbost. They were represented by able lawyers and Shaw who represented Donald Macrae asked the court how rioting could have taken place in Park when Douglas Thorneycroft, Mrs Platt's youngest brother was sharing his food and drink with the crofters. Duncan Macrae, son of the head keeper maintained that this was a crucial factor in determining the verdict – he may well have been right. After almost a two day trial the verdict was that all accused were innocent of all charges brought against them. This verdict had far reaching consequences, not only in Lewis but throughout the Highlands because it made oppressive landlords realise that they could no longer impose their tyrannical will against the people and expect the backing of the law.

Donald Macrae who had done so much for the people of Lochs, did not stay very long after the Park Deer Raid, leaving Balallan in Spring 1889 perhaps feeling that he had achieved his goal in Lochs and that there were pastures new where he could further his aim to achieve Land Law Reform. The last entry he made in the school log book was: "I opened the school today for the last time. I spoke to the children at 1pm and I advised them to be truthful, honourable and diligent in their profession. To give honour to anyone, whoever it was if his behaviour deserved honour; to strive to win everyone's goodwill and not to fear anyone or anything but only to fear evil. With that I bade them goodbye".

The following poem was written by me in the name of the Lochs heroes who partook in the raid of defiance against the landowner in 1887.

REUD NA PAIRCE
le Gaisgich nan Loch (1887)

THE PARK DEER RAID

'Se bhochdain is an eu-ceart
A rinn ar daoine lèireadh.
'Sa dh'fhàg sinn ann an èiginn
Le acras is gach cruadal.

It was poverty and iniquity,
That caused our people pain,
And left us in dire straits
With hunger and with hardship:

Ach thàinig curaidh feumail
A sheas ar cùis gu treubhant'
MacRath bha cho lèirsinneach
Is chuir ar strì an òrdugh.

But a useful hero came,
Who bravely stood our cause,
Macrae who was so bright
And he organised our strife.

Thug e dùlan dhàn Riagh'ltas
Ged chosgadh e bhith-beò dha
Is chuir e ann an rian dhuinn
Dòigh sam faigheadh sinn fuasgladh.

He defied Authority
Though it could cost him dear,
And he organised for us a way
Which made our path so clear

Ged bha chùis glè dhòrainneach
Cha robh geilt no uamhas air
Oir chuir e ann an dìmeas
Gach lagh a rinn an uachd'ran.

Although the matter was perplexing,
He felt not fear nor terror,
Because he showed complete contempt
For the edicts of the landlord.

Air madainn mhoich Di-màirt dhuinn
Gun thog sinn oirnn don Phàirce
Is ann an sin bha lèir-sgrios
Air na fèidh a bh'anns an àite.

Early on a Tuesday morning,
We set off for Park Forest,
And what a slaughter was there
Of the deer that were in that place!

Is thug sinn iomadh ionnsaigh
Air damh donn nan cròicean
Is sinne bha gu suaimhneach
An cois Airigh Dhòmhnaill Chaim.

We made many attacks,
On the antlered red stags
And how happy we were
Beside the shieling of Dòmhnall Cam*

Bha pàilliun ann 's bha òrain
Bha conaltradh is spòrs ann
Bha damh slàn ga ròsdadh leinn
'S bu chùbhraidh bha am fàileadh.

There were tents and there were songs,
There was conversation and also fun;
We had a whole stag roasting,
And how sweet was the aroma!

*One-eyed Donald Macaulay from Uig.

The coin that Donald S Macdonald (Doilidh a' Bhèiceir) of 52 Balallan, hit − Arrow indicates mark from bullet

Chapter 12

The Homing Half-Crown and the Joys of Motoring

The abridged version of Jaques' speech at the front of the book could in parts refer to most of us. I try to make myself believe that I am not yet – at 84 years of age – beyond stage 6, because I can read a car number plate without glasses at 25 yards, I still have some of my own teeth, and I have good taste as my wife Margaret will corroborate, and therefore I am not 'sans everything' but 'avec tout'.

In such a frame of mind I will conclude my Memoirs on a cheerful note as I recall some amusing and amazing characters from my younger days in Balallan.

Stick a half-crown into the face of a peat bank and try to score a bulls-eye on it at 40 yards with a .22 rifle. Perhaps it sounds impossible, but that feat was achieved back in 1931 by Donald S Macdonald (Doilidh a' Bhèiceir) of 52 Balallan. He was then an 18 year old youth and had chanced on Malcolm J Macleod (Calum Iain Anna Ruaidh) of 69 Balallan and Hector Macaulay (Eachann a' Ghrosair) of 33 Balallan who were having target practice.

At Doilidh's first shot the half-crown disappeared into the peat bank, much to Calum Iain's chagrin whose half crown it was! However, it was eventually dug out but despite efforts to restore the half crown to its pristine state the dent of the .22 bullet was left just off-centre on its face. Shortly after this incident Calum Iain parted with the coin.

Present also at the scene were Roderick John Mackenzie of 54 Balallan and myself who would be 8 years and 7 years of age respectively. I was not very impressed by the marksmanship of Dolidh because I did not know any better, but I was very impressed when the half-crown was retrieved from about a foot inside the face of the peat bank!

In the meantime Doilidh continued to show his superb shooting ability, with both rifle and shotgun, and as I lived at that time in our home at 50 Balallan – 2 crofts away – I was aware of some examples that impressed me a great deal.

One incident comes to mind when some geese alighted in Bealach Seadail more or less directly above his home and Doilidh stalked them, which was no easy task as there was little cover. However, with his double-barrelled shotgun he brought down two and winged another when they rose. The injured bird flew away to end up in a hole in an underground burn behind the hills above Loch Cuthaig. Shortly afterwards as it happened, Angus Maclean of 51 Balallan was passing by there while he was taking his cow to her grazing and he was mystified to hear the cackling of a goose but could see no bird in the vicinity. Angus was not superstitious but his hearing was good and he soon located the bird, wrung its neck and like the Israelites of old gave thanks for the manna, this time not from Heaven but from an underground burn!

After World War Two broke out Doilidh joined the Army and served with the Cameron Highlanders in the UK, Middle East, North Africa and Italy. After he was demobilised he took over as merchant in his father's shop at 52 Balallan and on one occasion when he was checking the takings for the day in the mid-fifties, he noticed an odd looking half crown. He blinked ... and blinked again and his mind flew back to a day in 1931 and a peat bank at the West End of Balallan. There among the silver was a half crown with an off-centre dent on its face. The date on the coin was 1923 – common currency in 1931. There can never be any positive proof that it was the peat bank half crown but the circumstantial evidence points that way! Where was it during the intervening quarter century? Needless to say Doilidh was determined that the half crown would not wander again and so he carried it about with him in his driving licence holder. After his demise in 1998 his daughter Joan took possession of the half crown which is still a cherished family memento.

Once upon a time there lived in Balallan a delightful raconteur known as 'Monty' who told delightful stories which were never directed abusively against anyone. He was a self-effacive character who never wished to offend anyone except himself. In Lewis when Communion Services were held it was customary for 'strangers' from all over the Island to congregate to the location of the Services, especially at the weekend and stay with anyone who invited them. It was customary in those days to have a special breakfast on Sunday morning consisting inter alia of bacon and eggs. A Harrisman happened to call on Saturday evening at Monty's house and he was made welcome as was the wont. On Sunday morning when the housewife had dished out an appetising breakfast of bacon and fried eggs, Monty asked his guest to say grace. The Hearach duly obliged but instead of a grace it was a peroration he made and by the time he was finished the plates were covered with congealed grease. Monty was too polite to remonstrate and off they went to church when breakfast was over.

When church dismissed, the Hearach tagged on to Monty and off they went on the two-mile trek to Monty's home. Monty asked the Hearach when they were about a mile-and-a-half from his house if he would come with him to dinner. The Hearach immediately agreed and Monty turned to him and said: "That's fine, but start the grace now!"

In pre-World War Two days, the village Post Office was located at 20

Balallan and the mail came by van from Stornoway. The village postman was Donald Macmillan 51 Balallan (Donald of the 'White Horse' cure mentioned earlier) who would meet the mail van and start his round by first delivering the mail to the West End of the village by foot. This meant that residents to the east of the Post Office would have to wait until Donald returned from his West End delivery trip before his East End deliveries began to their homes. Consequently many of the males east of the Post Office would assemble at 20 Balallan to collect their mail on its arrival from Stornoway. During good weather an open-air meeting would take place where some individual would take the opportunity to pontificate on some subject that appealed to him.

One sunny morning Murdo Mack who was present and who wished to express his conception of Astronomy drew everyone's attention to the sun which shone in all its glory in the South East and he remarked " When I got up this morning that sun was just rising above the horizon, but look where it is now and by evening it will have set in the West. Tomorrow morning it will rise again in the East; is the work of creation not wonderful?" The late Murdo John Macdonald 14 Balallan then a senior student in The Nicolson Institute Stornoway ventured to set the record right by stating that the sun did not move, that it was the earth that was moving, and he further explained how this affected our sunrises and sunsets.

Murdo Mack turned to him and sadly said to him; "Murdo John, if that is what they are teaching you in Stornoway it is high time you came back home!"

Shades of Christopher Columbus!

Nowadays many motorists have Satellite Navigation systems or SatNav installed in their vehicles and instances have been reported of people getting hopelessly lost and ending up in the back of beyond having apparently followed the precise instructions given by their SatNav in order to reach their destination.

In Balallan in the Fifties a simpler method was used. One just stopped and asked. So it was on this particular day when some tourists were driving through the village. They chanced upon another local worthy as he was out and about as usual studying the traffic through the village.

"Can you tell us the way to Gravir?" they politely enquired.

Now those familiar with the area will know that Balallan is a very long village which lies on the north side of Loch Erisort and that the road to South Lochs joins the Balallan road at the head of the Loch. This junction was commonly referred to locally as 'Ceann a' Rathaid'. From there the road meanders along the south side of Loch Erisort in the opposite direction going through the various villages there including Gravir. Quick as a flash our worthy issued the directions they had requested "Go to Ceann a' Rathaid and then reverse for 13 miles!"

Chuir mi a'bhàrdachd a leanas ri chèile aig an Nollaig 1995 agus le sin tha mi a'toirt an oidhirp seo gu crìch

GU MÀIREAD

Thàinig mi don t-seòmar chadail;
Bha thu'n sin nad chadal sèimh,
Bha do ghruaidhean mar na ròsan,
D'anail gluasad gu sìobhalt rèidh;

Bha do mhuineal mhìn-gheal chuimir,
Mar an canach air bhàrr nan sliabh,
Bha do shùilean dùint' fod fhrasgan,
Thu cho àillidh 'sa bha thu riamh.

Sheas mi tacan beag gad choimhead
Is ghluais mo smuain gu làithean cian -
Chun na h-oidhche chur sinn seachad,
Cùl cruaich-mhòna gu èirigh grèin.

Gus an latha thug sinn bòidean
Gum biodh sinn còmhladh fad ar rèis,
Gun dìreadh sinn a' bheinn le chèil'
'S gun trialladh sinn le chèile sìos.

Bha an dìreadh cneasd is àghmhòr
Is sinn a'sireadh dùthaich àrd,
Sinn a' mealtainn laithean aigneach
Air slighe na beinne suas gu bàrr.

Sin far robh an sealladh bòidheach
H-uile latha na b'fheàrr na càch,
Sin far'n d'fhuair sinn iomadh sòlas
Sonas glòirmhòr an caidreabh gràidh.

Nis tha tìm air gabhail seachad,
Is thàinig caochladh air ar deann,
Ach tha'n t-astar sìos a' bhruthach
Nas luaith na clach a'ruith le gleann.

Nuair a ruigeas sinn an abhainn
'S gum faigh sinn sàbhailt oirre null,
'S e mo ghuidhe sinn gun tachair
Air na raointean tha fada thall.

Rough Translation

I composed this poem at Christmas 1995 and with that I will now sign off.

TO MARGARET

I came into the bedroom,
There you were sound asleep,
Your cheeks were like roses
Your breath moving slowly and deep.

Your smooth-white handsome bosom
Was like cotton-sedge on high slopes
Your eyes were closed beneath your lashes
You were as beautiful as aye you were.

I stood a-while to watch you
And my mind sped back to days of yore;
To the night we spent together
Behind a peat-stack till early dawn.

To the day we gave our vows
That we would spend our days together
That we together would climb the hill
And that together we would descend.

The climb was pleasant and very happy,
As we sought a higher plane;
We enjoyed many happy days,
On the journey to the summit.

What a beautiful sight was there,
Every day surpassing others;
That's where we enjoyed much solace
Glorious days in love's embrace.

Now that time has passed on,
And our pace has changed,
But the journey down the slope
Is fast as a rolling stone down a glen.

When we arrive at the river
And we can safely get across
My plea is that we meet again
On the plains that are far beyond.

John M Macleod with his sisters, Annie and Sophia above, and below the family's house at 50 Balallan where he lived until he was married